About the Author

Nawres Chikhaoui is a Possibilitarian-Mindset coach who was born and raised in Tunisia. In 2018, she moved to the UAE to pursue her dream of becoming a cabin crew member, relying on her strong intuition and burning desire. After achieving many micro and macro goals, she wrote her first book *Cabin Crew – The Luminaries*, which proves that dreams can be achieved with steadfast consistency and self-belief. This led her to become a voracious reader and a loyal member of the personal transformation field. Today, Nawres is the founder of Run It, an educational platform that provides programs which help shape lives in the personal enrichment and empowerment world.

Nawres' vision extends to public speaking, and she is devoted and committed to her own race and mighty mission of helping you realize your true gift, achieve your goals, and eventually run your life on your own terms.

"In this man-made world, nothing is impossible because you are the Possibilitarians."

Run Your Race

Nawres Chikhaoui

Run Your Race

Olympia Publishers
London

www.olympiapublishers.com
OLYMPIA PAPERBACK EDITION

Copyright © Nawres Chikhaoui 2024

The right of Nawres Chikhaoui to be identified as author of
this work has been asserted in accordance with sections 77 and 78 of
the Copyright, Designs and Patents Act 1988.

All Rights Reserved

No reproduction, copy or transmission of this publication
may be made without written permission.
No paragraph of this publication may be reproduced,
copied or transmitted save with the written permission of the publisher,
or in accordance with the provisions
of the Copyright Act 1956 (as amended).

Any person who commits any unauthorised act in relation to
this publication may be liable to criminal
prosecution and civil claims for damage.

A CIP catalogue record for this title is
available from the British Library.

ISBN: 978-1-80439-372-7

This is a work of fiction.
Names, characters, places and incidents originate from the writer's
imagination. Any resemblance to actual persons, living or dead, is
purely coincidental.

First Published in 2024

**Olympia Publishers
Tallis House
2 Tallis Street
London
EC4Y 0AB**

Printed in Great Britain

Dedication

To the racer who dwells within all of us, the racer whose grit is unstoppable, the racer who never gives up.

Acknowledgments

To bring this book to life has been an act of extreme courage, dedication, and effort. Despite all the low lows and high highs, I've kept going for two years. For that, I have many to thank: To my parents, thank you for committing your races a million times over to raise us. You're the power and love I run with. To Grace, my cat. You're my daughter. Thanks a ton for sitting on my lap and tampering with the keyboard while I wrote these pages. Your presence in my life is like my must-have pillar. I'm extremely appreciative of my readers for picking up this book. Thank you for trusting me and most importantly for believing in that racer inhabiting every one of you. My gratitude also goes to my caring and trustworthy friends. Without your constant support and encouragement, I would never be able to gather my thoughts and silence the inner doubting voices. Thank you for always pushing and calling me "A Fighter" and standing by my side mainly during those downbeat days when nothing seemed to be moving. The cover book picture was clicked at "Manej Horse Farm" in Cappadocia, Turkey, so a special salute must be credited to their staff, and Samed, the photographer, and his team. Finally, thank you to the editors at Olympia Publishers for working wholeheartedly on this work of love and for giving me the scope to deliver my message.

"Each of us has music that must not be stifled within us."
  – Robin Sharma

"Creating the life you want can be scary. But do you know what's scarier? Regret."
  – Jim Kwik

"When will you feel ready to race? You won't. It takes a leap of faith. Signing up for an ultramarathon takes a jump into the unknown."
  – Michael D'aulereo

"I wish I tested my limits and became an ice dancer. I wish I finished my studies and did something serious out of my chained talents, so I could stand on the independence line. I wish I pursued my dreams and didn't listen to them." Lost in thoughtfulness, Mom told me once.

With curiosity and resentment, I questioned her, "Mom, why did you just wish while you could do it?"

"Darling, I wish I were like you. Just like this, so fearless, determined, and outspoken. But I was that tongue-tied girl and too timid to stand for my rights. My family was discouraging. Much of that didn't exist in our belief systems. Our time was different then. What's normal nowadays was extreme. I wish I were a lion and refused to walk with them.

"And you know very well that I had to give up on school so I could take care of your uncles and aunt. When I was done with that, it was the age as per the 'society' to get married and so your grandmother proposed to me your father. Ever since I've been committing my lifetime to and for you.

"I had to follow my parents' instructions blindly and I wish I didn't. I can't blame them because they didn't know better. It was also my mistake that I didn't fight for what I believed I could be. I wish…

"I take it a little easier at times, but my day-to-day life is about that butchering nagging guilt. Psychologically, it is tough. Really tough. I feel that I have given so much to others and very little to myself," she added.

I just went numb listening to her. My heart sank and was banging hard when I heard that. Every word fell into my stomach like a smoldering fire.

As she noticed my dejected face, she smiled widely and continued, "But, at least, I have you now. You are the greatest gift that I have in this world. You are the best thing that ever happened to me. Seeing you doing what you love is my victory. I have this feeling that maybe my Deity is reimbursing it all through you. You're my hope."

Putting her arms around my shoulders, she said, "You're meant to do and not wish."

If your race has been taken from you and you've been surely living with sweaty guilt, then I've written this book for you.

Or if you simply want to unleash that beast within you and learn how to live a life of significance, this book is for you too.

That said, *Run Your Race* is for the peerless racer who dwells within all of us and refuses to give up.

Having traveled to Cappadocia, Maldives, Zanzibar, Milano, and Mauritius, I handcrafted and polished it to the best of my abilities.

Unequivocally believing in the horsepower which for me represents freedom, wisdom, dominance, valor, victory mastery, divinity, and peace, the cover book picture was shot in "The Land of Beautiful Horses," Cappadocia, Turkey.

The idea for this book popped up and sparked inside my mind two years back. It struck a chord, and I can't but thank my consistency and diligence for making it come to pass.

It was a dream which made my life worthwhile.

At times, I felt every bit as powerless and strongly tempted to just give up on everything around me, but I pressed ahead, and was eager to execute my mighty mission and desire in this world: seeing all of us able to unlock the door to whatever we wish ourselves to be, to become the person we've been dreaming of becoming. My mother's story and that of so many others has been my catalyst. As they say, "Stories move people," and I have used that as my motivation to write this book for you. I'm sharing my own personal run that has been clearly defined, bright, and strong, filled with restlessness and perseverance. I've faltered and had ups and downs, but never gave up and learnt my lessons the bloody hard way.

[I haven't won a Nobel prize or climbed the deadliest mountain. I have simply found my race and am running it with all the passion and focus that it desires.]

I'm bringing everything I've learned on the ride I've taken to get me here and reach a level where I can provide adequate knowledge that will help you unshackle that gift bestowed to you from heaven.

It's symbolically representing a culmination of wisdom and experience, and buzzing with the energy of both; endings and new beginnings.

I am helping you shed everything that no longer serves you and your wildest dreams. To reach inside and get inner understanding, so you stretch into your best version forward and rise with a sense of purpose, focus, change, and hope.

You might be familiar with the content, but are you doing it? I am here to persuade and guide you into what already exists deep inside you. To go deeper and force those dormant wishes and desires to the surface.

As a clarification, this is not a "do this" or "do that" book. This is more of sharing my stories and lessons, so I help you buy time because time is money.

To elaborate, making you a second version of me has never been my game. Rather guiding you to gain clarity is.

Writing this book doesn't also mean I have figured everything out. Life is a never-ending lesson, but we don't need to feel overwhelmed by it. We simply need to be what we deserve to be. And just to be where we need to be.

The guidance is for you and me. I need these pages as much as you do, so I allow Nawres to remind herself every day of what she's meant to be, what she's capable of, and importantly her WHY that she wakes up for daily.

Today is the call that you shouldn't miss. So, have a think. You know calls are hard to come by!

The Invisible Contract

"The most destabilizing thing for anyone is to have their core beliefs challenged. We feel better with the certainty of missing than the misery of uncertainty."

– Virginia Satir

The racer shall perform the terms and conditions set out in this contract:

Failing to fulfill the requirements, he/she shall be outcasted and the race will be confiscated.

- The racer is not eligible for building a career that unleashes his/her inner true potential and gets him/her to protrude. Doing so is considered a case of infringement.

The racer has to find a job, purchase a car, and get married to be content. Bringing another form of gratification is an atonement and not acceptable.

- The racer has to adopt the common path and footsteps.
- The racer has to believe and accept both superstitions of "age" and "genius."
- The racer has to abandon all forms of personal leadership.
- This contract guarantees its holder a basic and comfortable life.
- The racer shall inform the associators of each amendment to his/her thoughts and decisions, and obtain an agreement.
- The racer has no right to express or build another set of beliefs but the one created for him/her.

• The racer has to run along with the rest. Doing the opposite is a form of veering off.

As a consequence of the above, the racer shall not join or assemble another race.

It requires courage, grit, tremendous passion, and dedication to fathom and sign out from a contract none of us neither signed nor read.

It requires strength to dispel this huge cloud on the heart.

I trust this: none of us agreed to be a part of this heavy debt.

Awareness didn't appear then.

If it meant the slightest chance of being, I had no trouble deciding and terminating such an assignment. I had no issues giving up on its irrelevant liabilities and rights. I did not belong.

Having made this choice, the soul has become happier. The fate has been altered…

The race has been found… I resigned.

How about you?

It's time I believe to go after your dreams!

The clock is ticking, and the world is watching. Your race is on…

Chapter 1

Through Fire and Water. Through Earth and Heaven

"Patience with perseverance leads to us fulfilling our goals."
— Hector Garcia and Francesc Miralles

Dateline: June 2022

Being a dreamer and a supreme hour opportunist doesn't permit that much fun and sleep. JOMO is the air I am bound to breathe. It seems!

I desired this read to be different, potent, and unique in terms of its content, message, and cover. I had an idea and peerless faith in it.

"How could I possibly connect and speak about the book idea through its cover?" I interrogated myself.

With this first question, I decided to use horses as a symbol for what it includes from potencies.

It's no less true that they are the strongest. They can leap over hurdles and gallop hard for hundreds of thousands, perhaps for millions of miles.

They show you how to recognize true compatibility, embrace challenges, and take the leap.

In other words, they show you how to RUN YOUR RACE.

Something about it had remained popping and hitting at me, that I had to trust and adhere to.

There was a reason behind that idea. It was in my gut and brain.

I knew that it would prove itself. And somehow, I had to translate this idea into reality.

One fine night, I was scrolling through Instagram when I came across the official page of "Manej Horse Farm." It's the one farm for horse riding practice in Cappadocia, Turkey, and that led me on the path of finding this: the etymology of the word "Cappadocia" is "KATPATUKA," which means the land of beautiful horses.

Going back to ancient times, the Paleolithic period (Old Stone Age), Cappadocia used to breed strong horses.

"WHOA, you've got this, girl," I screamed at the top of my lungs. I was jumping and bubbling with enthusiasm.

This dream was all I could see. I dedicated my whole existence to it.

I worked on the idea as hard as I could for as long as I could; I made up my mind and commitment for that a long time ago. In June 2021, I found the shooting spot, contacted the photographer, chose the right outfit, and game-planned the manuscript and photoshoot to be completed in June 2022. Even though I had no idea about the chapters that I would write to back up my WHY. But one thing I knew for sure was that I was determined to make it actually happen. I grew restless in its pursuit. I vividly remember how the title was written everywhere in my notebooks, "Run Your Race."

I projected the result of that vision in my mind so clearly that the image pulled me towards it every day.

As far as I was concerned, there was no time to waste. My mind had been hardwired for two years, knowing that it would be a hell of a tiring journey from my first book *Cabin Crew – The Luminaries*. I also knew that one way to make the commitment happen was to go through it all passionately with steadfast focus.

One day after the other, I was smashing deadlines and unclipping insignificances and distractions. I lost count of those dedicated moments I spent on the manuscript with barely any rest as I was working almost every day. I would push myself every morning with the sun up no matter how much my body wanted a good sleep, so I could fit a few hours of writing into my day even when it was impossible.

I retold the goal to myself regularly and kept my "I can" above anything else.

Time flew by and I completed the first manuscript as prearranged.

Luck doesn't exist in my book of life and I know this from my experience: if you want something, the whole world will start to work miraculously for you. And that's the divine truth.

Alas, a slaughtering physical agony came uninvited. I couldn't feel my body. I was crashing and my legs just gave up on me. The ache was real. My body was in a chaotic state.

Stress advised me to skip the idea. At first, I thought of canceling the photoshoot, but when I glanced at the goals board and saw the book title out there, shining and beaming on the list, I gathered my thoughts.

I was sick. Every muscle begged me to stop. I could barely walk at that time. Still, I made a stand for my calling and went through my plan.

As the plan had to keep me on a trip, I had to manage it my way.

The phone rang at two p.m., startling me. I couldn't stand at first but had to consider another grueling trip to the airport.

My energy ran out and I couldn't leave my mission incomplete, so I was confused about how to convince someone consistent like me. I thought about how far I had come. Sleepless, fatigued, and tired as a nightmare I went and caught the flight to Istanbul. I reached my destination late at night and managed to rest for four hours at the hotel.

Felt a sense of relief getting my feet on the ground, but not for so long as I had another flight to catch on the same day.

"If you're going through hell, keep going. Why would you stop in hell?"

— Steve Harvey

As I boarded the aircraft to Cappadocia and flew there, the pain hit me harder in my feet again. My body was screaming, but the idea screamed louder. Truly, acting with purpose makes the most difference in the world. I was driven.

It was more than a warning sign. I had serious chronic physical fatigue due to sleep deprivation and barometric air pressure. I could hear my veins and every tension crying.

That week, I hated "flying" for what it did to my body. June 2022 was cruel and crazy.

The only thing that could defend the hustle and dedication was this: I have a dream. A message to deliver. Limiting beliefs to change. People to help.

My consistency hassles me sometimes. I know.

After almost two hours of delay, we landed safely. Seeing it was midnight on my watch got me recalling that the photoshoot would start at four a.m., and that drove me insane. I was short on time. To illustrate, I was left with no time to rest and recover.

Another million thoughts came in.

Not knowing the hotel's location and its distance from the airport, I ran and grabbed the first taxi.

"That's one hour and a half driving, madam," said the taxi driver.

I gasped in frustration, but I had no choice and so agreed, cursing myself while being inaudible to anyone else.

"Let's go."

Four hours later:
Cappadocia felt wonderful. It was a heavenly place to visit. I had never seen such divine beauty in my life. It is a region like no other in the world. It is exceptional and full of wonders.

We stopped by the Love Valley at first to click some

memorable pictures since it was on our way. As I looked around, little cupcakes of happiness moved beneath me.

With the sun starting to cast its soft light and gentle breeze, the fire balloons marked their journey to the bewitching sky. They seemed to be flying. The mountain tops and caves were bathed in orange light. A little later, girls from all edges could be seen catching the sights at every turn of the cameras with their long colorful dresses.

The atmosphere was just phenomenal. It was startlingly beautiful. Super grand.

Heading to the farm and seeing the staff preparing for the horses made me feel better.

The camera lights came on and I just looked straight ahead, for a moment, lost in thought, and by the sun breeze, feeling a part of me being proud.

I needed to whack the pain and hold myself with every click as my energy was draining.

My heart was burning fire. Still, there was suffering. Just know, that this challenge was a disaster. It was a daymare. I had every painful physical feeling. I barely spoke and felt the clock was ticking slowly. Truly, I wanted to shoot myself.

I was all alone in my struggle and that's when you learn how to muster the effort to pull off the impossible.

And because I had a vision, I didn't quit. I was managing. Barely. At least, I was on my mission. It had to be and that fueled me enough to finish what I started.

The thing is, most people give it up immediately to their pain, whether it's mental or physical. And when you feel either of these, remember that you always have the choice. It's the choice of embracing and welcoming all experiences.

If I succumbed that day, you probably wouldn't be reading this book. I'm serious.

It goes without saying that I did all this after a sleepless night.

But apparently, I look fresh on the cover and that's thanks to Helen, my make-up assistant, and her raw talent.

I wished the stay was a little longer, but another flight getting me back to Istanbul was calling at four a.m.

And don't you think I slept after the photoshoot before my next trip because I didn't. My heart took me on a Green Tour that made me rich in mind and soul.

I had faced challenges that I had met head-on. All meshed together in harmony.

Each challenge seemed to be tougher than the other. It appeared to be never-ending.

You know, giving up wasn't an option. Sharing another secret: something didn't click as I finished and polished the first manuscript of this book you're holding now. I felt something missing and I couldn't pinpoint it but my intuition did, and yes eventually the sample got rejected from one of the publishers. They wanted a non-fiction book written in a narrative form.

"Dear Nawres,

Our team reviewed your work, but I'm sorry to say that we're not able to take you as an author at this time… Your work definitely has a lot of potential, but we're looking for something with more of a narrative structure."

After reading this, I felt something deep inside, strong enough for my heart to say: "This is what was hard for me to explain when I submitted the work."

Honest. I doubted each chapter. I thought to surrender and that terrified me. I feared throwing this read in the dustbin. I sat on the bed unsettled, trying to calm the ego and those pessimistic thoughts.

I went into a flashback. During those strenuous and arduous times, I sat at the table scripting and smashing deadlines as the opportunities I had abandoned just gleamed as a harsh memory in front of me.

Working halfway dear racers sometimes doesn't guarantee you halfway.

I burst into tears and somewhat managed to sleep for a couple of hours before going sleepless for the rest of the night. That's the case when you continue being led by your emotions. You will only be sinking in sheer pain and vexation. That's what happens when you deny this: our emotions are the cause of our thinking.

The unease increased. I went crazy looking for something I could distract myself with. I couldn't open a book to read or connect the headphones and get my body moving. There was no motivation, no mood.

"Halftime" [a documentary film which talks about the career of Jennifer Lopez] had just been released. Something pushed me to watch it as if it was a sign.

An icon and tempo genius like JLO has been fighting for decades to be recognized regardless of all her success and achievements.

I thought to myself, "How can you possibly give up? Is this how you're going to help people?"

Her words and message came over me that night like a sparking inspiration. And I woke up the following day with a realization that hit me like thunder. "Ditzy, you're a fighter. Giving up isn't for you," I said to myself.

I'd had many such rejections, delays, and disappointments before. It's like I was already an expert at gathering my shattered pieces, and chaotic thoughts. Always finding my way.

I had to leave the ghosts of "failure" far behind.

Instead of asking myself, "Am I able to do this?" I silenced any talk of the worst and asked myself, "How can I make this book better? How can I dig even deeper in my message?"

I knew that there was a better and more productive way of writing it.

You might be asking yourself now, "In which way was this book written?"

It was filled with mantras, tips, and tricks. I inserted the words "racer" and "run your race" a million times over. There was more about directing you and very little about me and my raw and tough seasons.

I completely forgot this powerful advice from Arfeen Khan:

"When you meet people and they ask you to introduce yourself, there has to be a story attached to it. Because if I say, "Ladies and gentlemen, for the past ten years, I have done absolutely nothing in my life and now I am going to teach you how to make a fortune; you would ask me to get lost!"

The rejection was actually the perfect place and redirection from which I had to give up on what was good for what's now I believe to be the best for you.

Maybe I would never reach your hearts and souls (I pray I am doing so). Maybe you would never be able to dive with me into my messy, determined, and hard-earned race.

Bruised, lost in despair but with the desire to re-start it all over again; I opened the laptop to see the schedule and pick whatever I had from my off days and rest periods, squeezing the free time to its absolute best.

Psychologically, the route felt never-ending, and finishing this work seemed forever out of reach.

It took every bit of strength to gather my thoughts and script everything again. I didn't know where to start next, but I knew one thing: The race had to continue.

So much did hit me even more during the rewriting process.

I pushed so much in an unimaginable way. Logging off from the world and keeping myself steady, focused, and grounded which I believe is the toughest. And so, I rewrote this book within forty days.

The journey of writing this read has shown me the truth about who and what I am. I was not the same person when I finished both samples. It changed me beyond my imagination.

I feel fortunate and wholesome even after crossing sharp fences.

I confess… each barrier I confronted and sweat drop I drained has blessed me with fascinating assets of realization and growth. Telling you all of this is not a promotion or plug for the book.

I am telling you all of this because whatever race you take and run in life is not going to be full of ice cream, chocolates, and candies. You will still have to experience a lot of impediments and obstacles.

The moment you embark on your excursion for that vision, there are going to be humps and dips, uneven and slippery roads. The obstacles are being put but to test your faith and seriousness. To refine your art, hasten your commitment, strengthen your self-discipline, and reveal your unseen aptitudes. To model and shape you for something even greater.

As I am writing this, I recall Santiago from *The Alchemist* [Paolo Coelho's novel] and the uplifting coaches as the dream assailants he meets, the girl he falls in love with, the upheavals he navigates, the lessons he learns, and even the maddening emotions he feels. Everything happens as he decides to chase his dream. He ends up not just finding the treasure but his true self too.

Those unlimited challenges could throw me off obviously.
But it didn't.

And if you would ask me "Why are you doing this to yourself?", I would tell you because I am a dreamer and for my dreams, I will go through fire and water, through earth and heaven.

Following your dreams will make you do crazy things and cost you a lot.

To add weight to this idea, allow me to share with you my journey of becoming a life coach.

It wasn't the "I can do everything" hypothesis. Rather it was the burning desire and strong will buried deep inside me.

Psychologically speaking, whatever leads to your needs becomes an addiction. Eventually, that's what happened.

I became addicted to every way that would lead me there. I did my research and approached every single experienced person. I became utterly obsessed with the idea.

Studying deeply the areas that would help me reach my purpose.

The course was expensive and to fit that with other liabilities was difficult.

Instead of widening the gap between where I was and where I wanted to be, I bridged it.

"Everyone is working and has challenges, so don't give a reason why can't you do it; you have to give a reason why you can do it."

— Arfeen Khan

I believed that I could make a road map and thus manage my finances. Soon enough, I found that my expenses had mounted. They were higher than my income: credit cards, loans, certifications, courses, and publishers to pay. There were months when I really couldn't pay it all.

Banks didn't stop calling me. The fatigue wasn't only mental and physical but also emotional.

I fumbled for a solution and felt financially insecure. I can say that it was a painstaking and bumpy procedure to get myself out of that swamp.

Did I sit and plan? No, and I am honest.

I took responsibility for what happened since I would rather feed "the outcome frame" and not "the blame frame." The event had happened already. Working on my reaction by controlling my thoughts was the first step. I wanted to save money obviously and that did clash with my need, the need of learning and investing in my mindset.

Here's the formula: study your needs and desires. Have a deep look and assess if both are matching or clashing. Make a list of what you truly need and start checking them off.

Let's take a situation as an example, you need to be fit, but you want to eat all day long. Or you want to be completely on your own in life but from the other side, you need a committed relationship. How ironic. Right?

Your needs sustain you. Your desires entertain you.

[You can know more about how to identify your values and what triggers different responses within you in the RUN IT coaching platform; just go here: run-it.ae]

I had to pay the price, and it was very heavy on my shoulders. I struggled to get myself out of the situation.

I asked God for a sign, an 'orange car.' I don't know how it popped up, but it did.

One day as I was back from work, an 'orange car' found its way and parked in front of mine.

I burst into tears. I felt guided and spiritually supported. That sign was aligned with the deep inner urge and there was no need to convince anyone else or keep feeding my fear of the unknown. **I EMBRACED THE EXPERIENCE. THE UNIVERSE HAD MY BACK.** In the end, it all worked out fine, and the worthy goal of growing for which I exhausted all the ways paid me off.

The truth is that it wasn't for the certification. It was and still is for the **INTENTION.** It's for what's sitting inside me. It's for the knowing sense and spiritual awakening that know what I'm capable of. It's for being of service and what I can do for the human race.

Even when life went tough and rough, I didn't stop. That's why you have to have a strong intention behind everything you do.

My motivation is intrinsic until this very moment.

Yeah. It was the risk of debt panel, but better than the risk of dying with a dream within.

My conscious mind would ask me every day, "Can't you see your reality?" And that's one of the dream killers if you are not assured and confident enough about your reason. Here's a fact: "Practicality is the absolute killer of all extraordinary dreams." In the words of Jen Gottlieb.

It doesn't matter what you know consciously. That's how you have been trained and what you have been told. What you see is very limited. For example, no one bothered to sign up for my very first workshop. I lost count of how many times I had to cancel it. That was a part of the journey then. Now I have the clients signing in for my courses. I was broke and more, and I am not that anymore. That's one of the biggest proofs that you're more than your NOW.

The idea is so powerful that I should give it its bold

message: **Your reality of today doesn't define your reality of tomorrow. Always remember this.**

And for another fact: what is going right for someone else doesn't mean that's right for you too. To illustrate, for the majority of people, investing in houses brings them happiness. Brilliant!

I have no judgment. It's a smart move to secure yourself financially as who knows what tomorrow may bring. Some others keep themselves committed to work for decades just because they have bills to pay.

For me as Nawres, the perceived safety or security is just an illusion; a suffocating force that kills what you can truly be. Investing in assets that grow in deep value like your mindset, skills, and health brings me happiness. Through that, I can have the financial security. Growing myself daily is my celebration. That's more than just money. It's the celebration of winning from the inside and developing the habit of success in your daily life.

And, thus the journey continued…

Soon, another rush was kicking in: the rush of opening RUN IT that I hold so close to my heart. I realized I wanted more than a second book. I wanted to create a platform; a virtual company for life coaching to make an impact and gather all the Possibilitarians together.

My "machine reality maker" [mind] was telling me often: You would go bankrupt again and end up on the street. You would turn out to be an embarrassment to your family. But something whispered in my ears again and told me that I was doing the right thing.

Please note that I'm not suggesting that you give up on all of your savings and leave yourself with nothing to bounce back on. But to "Listen to your heart. It's the best counselor there is." as Thomas L. Friedman said.

I was working and putting together everything I knew that could help the driven souls shape a transformational life, and this is how the platform was created. Making my own money was hard. In fact, very hard. I would fly, train, earn, invest in my vision, pay my loans (which were already taken for the same purpose), and then **REPEAT.** I would end up with no savings. And the more money I made, the more I invested in the platform quality to make it better.

We want the change and outcome, but are we willing for the trade-offs we have to make on the way?

The further I went in the pursuit of my **INTENTION**, the more roadblocks I had to face.

I woke up for years with absolutely nothing in my hands because nothing was moving on the outside and you will know that you are on the hardest path when things take time.

Here we can relate to The Compound Effect that Darren Hardy, the author, talks about. It's a principle of reaping massive results based on the small daily improvements you make that might seem insignificant and ungiving for now.

I have learned well that you can't grow a seed and harvest it tomorrow. The delays would make you feel like you are building on shifting sand. I have fathomed that there are things that you have to work on and others that you have to wait for, so you don't overwhelm yourself on the way. In the end, you will always see a harvest.

Indeed, they are all working together for you. So, if you're putting in the hour in this very moment, doing your best, beating procrastination, focusing on what you are good at, and making the small right choices, don't go double-minded. Remember this: The time you spend on your personal development is never wasted. For so many I sounded crazy to give up on the financial security for the sake of a potentially satisfying but unsure tomorrow.

I worked when there was no applause and no rewards. And I would still celebrate myself. I was happy with the baby steps and personal improvement I was making. I call them small victories up until today: every time I finish a chapter, work immediately on a new idea popping up, share what I learn, or stretch one of my skills, I turn out to be the happiest because I know that I'm guaranteeing myself a future full of possibilities.

I would challenge myself not to think of what was happening, so I would avoid expanding its energy in my life.

…And that's the biggest mistake most people commit when the shit hits the fan. They keep on repeating the story to themselves and those around them like a broken record until it goes even deeper into their lives. So why recreate your past? Why give energy to something negative and help it spread?

It has been a journey of intentional growth: a lot of risks, hard work, following through, learning, sacrifices, falling, rejection, closed doors, and making life-changing mistakes. In reality, growth comes often with a high price tag: a lot of goodbyes. Most people aren't willing to pay that price nowadays. They want the outcome but never the hustle. Even if you are willing to learn, know that without your commitment to change, nothing is going to happen.

Because you can't have new results with the same old way of thinking, same fellows, same habits, and same energy.

To break that "same," there is a lot to give up on. A lot to adopt. A lot to digest. A lot of "I don't feel like it" and you'll still have to do it. I say this because "impossible" is just a song victims love to play. Indeed, "The ones who look for the circumstances they want, and if they don't find them, they make them," as beautifully said by John C Maxwell. I am still reaching for more. Never dead to the possibilities. RUN IT is what I will grow through. That's my biggest motivation and development. A life commitment.

"Success in life comes not from holding a good hand, but in playing a poor hand well."
– Warren G. Lester

To anyone in need of reassurance, this is for you:

Stop centering your focus, time, and attention on the roadblocks and low lows. They will drain you. Remember why you are on this ride and how far you've come.

And don't think that dreams are just there to get us attached as they don't come true. That's not the case. A vision is brutally tough to attain and requires resilience and strength.

It has to seem unapproachable and ungiving, so we hold it even tighter.

And remember: Don't rush it and don't stall it either. Keep it slow, keep it escalating. Your dreams are not for nothing.

Chapter 2

Decide the Dead Time to Be Alive

"I see hope in the darkest of days, focusing on the brightest."
  – Dalai Lama

Thunderous news suddenly popped in: "UAE government to suspend passenger's flights in response to COVID-19."

As the pandemic began to multiply around the world, countries started restricting and sealing their territories.

Officially, on March 25, 2020, UAE's airports closed their doors and we had to shut our wings down.

Around the same time, businesses, schools, concerts, and indoor places had to order the masses to remain home so "Stay home, stay safe" became the new hashtag. Streets became deserted and "the significant other" became a threat to one another.

Financial setbacks, joblessness, rootlessness, and deaths happened. All within one month.

People had to let go of their possessions and savings to survive.

Truly, it was an emotional time marked by scarcity and unclarity.

The whole universe swooned in worried, hazy, and blurry time. And those high winds of insecurity had blasted and shattered peace, hopes, and dreams for our future.

I realized how messy and unpredictable life could be during the pandemic.

I had fathomed in those past years of serious financial crisis and instability this thing for sure: no one knows how the future is going to turn out. No one knows what would work and what would not. The truth is this: You can be big-headed today, but circumstances can change in the blink of an eye.

I knew importantly why we have to hope for the best and prepare for the worst.

Things have changed ever since and the media sprang as always into its mission: spreading horror among nations and bobbing us up and down.

"WHO declared ten thousand new cases, Coronavirus took over the lives of a thousand more, SARS COV-2 may continue for ages."

So much took a toll on our mental health and yet nobody but few talked about that.

I wished there was a better awareness rather than the one of "eat more garlic and ginger" and "maintain social distancing."

I wondered if the psychological immune system mattered as much for the media as the physical one.

I stood up one day and walked to the balcony to watch the neighbors lighting their phones screaming and singing. I didn't know whether they were celebrating or revolting the confinement.

But one thing I knew and made up my mind about in a moment was "The real precious commodity here is time."

I was blessed to not lose my job or be left on the street. Believe it or not, the dire financial consequences I had to face didn't bother me much. I cared mostly about my time and mental health.

Being a disbeliever in luck and a firm believer in creativity, vision, hard work, and creating opportunities where there are none. I couldn't do what everybody else was doing: going day by day complaining about what was lacking.

The world was governed by impractical people and I hated that. I hated starting my day at night and becoming a cyber zombie addicted to digital distractions. I wasn't that and couldn't bear it for long.

Re-forming walls into windows, my gut felt like kick-starting something within me: reading. Diving into such a new ritual was the best way to escape a dreadful reality positively.

I couldn't allow those eating their ripe harvest to pressure me into eating my seeds.

Scanning the situation seriously, I took care of my mental health more than anything else. I was logging myself out almost every day. I could calculate the hours I checked the news and social media platforms or the movies I watched. I wanted to protect my values enthusiastically.

The bullishness that started growing led me to sign in. All in.

And it wasn't just about hope. It was about that unexplained harmony with the good I desired for myself during such a dead time. It was about that creative promise and a chance to make myself a better person.

Putting the harrowing hours into learning made me a morning person: rising at five a.m.

I adopted the morning routine of world-builders from the same book that my heart pushed me to buy right before the pandemic "The 5 AM Club" by Robin Sharma (I call him a second father and not just a leadership expert).

I made another interesting decision which was working on my writing skills and scripting my first book *Cabin Crew*

– *The Luminaries*.

Time: four forty-five a.m.

Everyone was asleep. It was quite grim outside as the sun hadn't set its bountiful light on so far. The ant could be heard easily as the neighborhood was motionless.

"What the hell are you doing?" I vividly remember asking myself.

I couldn't scoop it up when I attempted at first to get up, but when I kicked the blanket away and made a second attempt, I woke up.

"In the morning when you rise unwillingly, let this thought be present: I am rising to the work of human beings. Why then am I dissatisfied if I am going to do the things for which I exist and for which I was brought into the world? Or have I been made for this, to lie under the blanket and keep myself warm?"
     – Marcus Aurelius

With eyes half closed and a struggle with how to sit in a "lotus position," I marked my first day of the 60 Days Challenge.

I made a quick dash later in the afternoon to the nearest typing center to buy a big whiteboard, print out some pictures I selected from the internet, and then returned to my place to start designing my first vision board ever.

The wise books, life-changing master classes, and long meditative and isolated hours inspired me to create it for its incredible ability to form thoughts into reality and banish on the way all sorts of disbelief (with serious effort of course).

It looked as promising and shining as my future and resembled the many achievements and happy moments, I've had so far.

I made my old room a collage of sticky notes filled with positive affirmations and far-reaching dreams. I was happy to build a safe inner world that I can even today go back into.

Every "five a.m." alarm set was a challenge and it annoyed me that I wanted to sleep. It was no joke and for that, I kept going.

Hydrating, meditating, visualizing, journaling, working out, reading, and then writing. That's how I had run my day for the fifty-nine remaining days that followed. That's how I have been up until today running my psychology, spirituality, physicality, and productivity. That's how I can be considered for consistency.

By shining a light on the new person I was building, the challenge was beginning to loosen a little, slowly, slowly.

There were those unpleasant and unforgiving reminders. I would fight at least with two to three negative ideas a day telling me that it was crazy thinking positively during such a perilously low time. That it was nonsense and useless. That I was chasing illusions. That aviation would never be back like before, and workplaces would get rid of more employees as we were barely operating some repatriation flights.

Still, I kept trying and achieving hits all the time. Small baby strides were stepped continuously.

Weeks and months on as I kept myself dedicated and focused, I was able to see the improvements and changes: the anxious breath became poised, the superficial understanding became profound and the average vocabulary became exceptional.

Interestingly, one book became two. Two became three and today I can proudly say this: As an avid reader, I have lost count of the number of books read.

I have reached happily to a position of writing I dreamt about and hoped to reach when I first had the idea. I was celebrating the progress though it was only visible to me.

I am here now writing for you due to that time which very few understood we had.

See, one minor action and decision led me to another outcome. And that's what I am always talking about. Follow your heart and intuition. They know you better. They see you farther.

It may seem surprising to say this, but the early days of isolation and deep crisis were some of my best times.

I had a perfect time, sitting and talking to myself, building an intimacy with it. Knowing what I wanted and what I didn't. I noticed things and triggered potentials I hadn't noticed in my previous years. I was building willpower and training my mind for what could be a tougher phase in life. My vision became sharper.

The epidemic truly made me fortunate enough: it made me feel richer than the richest.

Invoking the wisdom, there are a lot of turbulent, tough,

and chaotic times in the world. So much out there will try to put you off balance. There are so many reasons around to not take action.

The fact that I think you'll value is this: Life is a matter of choice.

The past itself is full of heroes who turned the upheaval into power:

Malcolm X had chosen prison to be his college: he decided to educate himself at a time when he was accused of being a criminal and was imprisoned for many years at a young age.

The same thing applies to Nelson Mandela and his memoir *Long Walk to Freedom* which was written in Robben Island.

"Hope was there and that is what helped us." Saying it after spending almost three decades of his life in jail.

If you've ever had an experience where you utilized the dead time and made it useful, I am proud of you. I salute you.

I am happy for every released artistic potential that found its path to the world, for the helping hands that were put out, for the lost souls who found some time to contemplate and understand themselves, for the workaholic who had time to rest and refuel the power, and for the splendid business ideas that came to pass during the epidemic.

That in my book of life makes you a "tempo genius." You've got this. I've got this. We've got this.

You too can make a change and let the dead time come alive. You can flourish regardless of your dead conditions.

Don't waste a turmoil that can help you rise later. Allow it to be your greatest time. Your secret ingredient. And let buoyancy be your "golden mask," your shining symbol in the gloom of tombs.

Imagine doing something for self-prowess, craft, health,

and surroundings whilst most people are still in bed watching reels, in doubt whether to order food or move on with sleep.

Imagine the inner gratification and heartening outcomes.

And get this: there is no right time. You choose the time to be right, inspiring, and unbeatable.

Exploit each second and bring the best out of it. Reverse the game and get the inside aura affecting the outside one this time.

I hope you have come to understand that the time you assumed to be dead, can help you run your race and reach mountain tops!

Chapter 3

Do the Hard Things First

"Do what is easy and your life will be hard. Do what is hard and your life will be easy."

– Les Brown

The Big Plan Page
It was early in my teenage years when I heard about the cabin crew job, but I didn't know much until I met a flight attendant based in the Middle East and shared an interesting conversation with her.

That day, I felt the alignment. Honest. I felt the discussion was a calling stressing the ultimate passion, purpose, and core values I have.

I would spend my days surfing through the net. I lived the whole scene in my mind. I knew that aviation would be the gateway to where I am today. That brings me to Robin Sharma's amazing quote: "Everything is created twice. First in the mind and then in reality."

The more I grew up, the more I knew it was what I wanted to be. The target was clear and the relevant plan too. No one could see that as it was all going behind the scenes. I kept it as a secret, a mission. Even when my friends or teachers shared stories about the occupation, I chose silence and pretended that the topic didn't matter while it was all burning deep inside me. I was serious about growing up and being what I am today.

Knowing that you can't be a crew without being a high

school graduate made me study very hard. And so, I made it with a good score.

The first obstacle was my age. I was still too young to be hired as the age required was still twenty-one for most airlines in the Middle East.

In the meantime, my personal relationship wasn't going well. My partner was trying to remake me: making me a second version of himself.

"Any plans for your studies?" he asked me once.

"I have a dream. I want to fly as a cabin crew and see the world. So, I am signing up for an English college," I replied happily.

"We will try to find something else for you," he added seriously.

This was the conversation that made up my mind to break up. He didn't respect my vision and so I lost my hope for the future we envisioned.

With a Razor-Sharp Focus, I Moved

I made it my number one focus to work on my English. I was proud that my score got me through one of the best government colleges for languages: "Bourguiba School."

That year, I had to live in a private dormitory as most colleges were located in the capital.

The rhythm of life away from home seemed to suit me though it was my first time staying away from my family. I had to be responsible for my studies, laundry, and cooking. All at once.

As I started putting on weight, I realized that I was taking a step back instead of forward towards my dream. We all know that to fly, you've got to be fit within a certain BMI.

So, the decision to lose weight was made and taken seriously.

I met a nutritionist and we set a plan in motion.

Needless to say, the journey of going slimmer was very tough on me, especially with exams and the rapid rate of the college courses.

But within four months of unwavering consistency, I lost thirteen kilograms while making it through my first year at college successfully.

It was the summer of 2018 when I was someone more ready and determined than before. I was closer to what I desired.

I thought nothing would happen at that time because I was still young and therefore had no choice but to carry on with the second year, believing it was the last at college.

Researching more about the recruitment events from home, I found that to be assessed for the cabin crew job, you would need to pay one of the aviation institutes which was something I couldn't afford. My expenses were already heavy on my father and I couldn't ask him for that huge amount.

What I did was home studying. I had the basic resources; a laptop and internet at home, so I believed I could teach myself and break the myth of that certificate. That hard work eventually did pay me off.

The Beginner's Luck

One day, while I was studying, my sister came in to break a game-changing news for me: "Do you remember my friend who used to work at the airport? I met her today by chance after almost seven years. She's been living in the Gulf ever since.

"We talked about you and I told her that you have grown up and now looking to live abroad to go and pursue your dream.

She has a job for you in the UAE. If you are willing to go, then you can make your way to your cabin crew thing."

[Here I keep your name confidential as you requested but I want to take a moment and thank you for opening UAE's door for me. You were a gift sent from God. You are not just a friend but a home away from home.]

I didn't believe her and replied with, "Truly I don't have time for your hilarity. Can't you see that I am studying?"

"Do I look like I am kidding, for God's sake? Think about it and then we can break the news to mom and dad. Deal?"

At that moment, I didn't believe myself. I had a bunch of mixed feelings roaming inside me.

I went speechless and felt the universe moving in a way that made me believe in magic and proved the credibility of the great old saying: "When the student is ready, the teacher appears."

It didn't take so long for me to say yes and accept the offer. I didn't think of what would happen next and whether my parents would accept it or not.

I had to trust my instinct and fight those critics and apish illusions of "you're too young, inexperienced, get graduated…" Apish illusions that I had to unfollow and trust my instinct instead.

I managed to convince Dad and Mom as I left them with a one-way thing: either I go or I go. It was my race and I wanted to run it.

Almost another month would pass before I finally received the visa. I jumped out of happiness and made a promise to myself that I would be back but with the dream achieved in my hands. That I would give it everything I had.

In the meantime, I was facing a very hard decision which was leaving my family and that was making my heart ache with pain.

I have a soft spot for my parents. They were and still are always there for me.

My mother was in tears as she didn't want to let me go, but she couldn't say it.

The day I was heading to the airport, my brother didn't know. He thought I was going to college to carry on with my studies. I didn't tell him because I knew he would stop and deny me of such an opportunity. I had the foresight and an entire action movie could be devoted to what for sure would happen if I told him (perception is projection). I protected my move and went in silence.

Fighting In the Warzones

So, instead of simply doing what everyone else did, which was paying for the aviation course and waiting for one of the airlines to conduct an open or assessment day, I did what was hard.

I moved to the UAE at the age of nineteen with nothing more than two hundred USD, a CV I struggled to create by myself, a business attire I borrowed from my sister, and a desire to pursue my teenage dream: The Cabin Crew Job.

Putting the ball firmly in my family's court has never been my game. I wanted to become entirely independent and dared to do that to the point of no return.

War I: "Being an Outcast"

Yes, I dropped out of college and decided to work as a purchaser abroad in a shoe market for a very low income (I lost half of my first-ever salary, not knowing until this very moment where it went).

And ever since, my journey has started.

Then, I had zero experience with what that job would bring

I bet you think there was a limousine waiting to pick me up from the airport to the seven-star Burj. Hell no!

Nothing from whatever I imagined matched the actual reality. Not even the lowest expectations. And that was my mistake because I prepared myself for pleasure but not for pain.

I forgot that there was a divine plan already set compelling me in a way to slow down, struggle, and learn.

For a start, I found that almost nobody was speaking English. Urdu was the only language used in that workplace which I knew less than nothing about.

There was no choice. To work with them, you would have to forget about your rich vocabulary and correct grammar. You would have to manage in all possible ways and deliver your message.

I was foreign myself. I was like a bird still learning how to open my wings and fly.

Talking to new people from all edges didn't come easily to me. It was the first time I was experiencing different cultures, habits, and personalities.

Dealing with diverse people taught me a lot about communication and interpersonal skills.

Working there, I was provided with accommodation that got me living in a room of eight people and sleeping on those high sleeper beds, more popularly known as "bed space."

The first night I saw the room, I felt bad and couldn't sleep. It was very small and congested. It was stupefyingly dull and had nothing else but a dark curtain and a cheap used mattress. I felt a bit of misery and poverty. Don't get me wrong. You might think that I was cut from a different cloth. But that wasn't the case. It's just that I thought it was a place that would promise me at least a bit of comfort. That it would offer me an escape from a very discouraging environment and bring hope. Only to find it queasy and stealing the comforting wind of privacy and serenity that I needed.

The idea of taking the top space and getting there every night didn't seem pleasing to me. It must have been written all over my face that I wasn't happy being there. However, I couldn't complain because there were no other options. It was either that or to sleep on the floor. By far, my mind was the one trying to convince me that it was a hard mission to fulfill at a time when I was already primed to do what was harder.

I thought to myself, "If you can't do this, how will you be able to get your dream job?"

I remember reading somewhere that nothing kills you or motivates you like your own mind. Yes. Here, I agree.

So, I had to crush it like any other negative thought and managed to bring the psychology to climb and descend daily.

There was another room in the same flat for five girls. So, we were in total thirteen girls working for the same company but for different departments.

Our numbers can justify why the bathroom was another hustle. It was used as per the slots: You would have to wait for your turn to get there and couldn't exceed fifteen minutes. The best time to use it without distraction was late at night.

For my clothes, there was a one-door steel wardrobe with some hangers. I placed what I could fit from my stuff and kept the rest in my trolley bag.

And I can't forget about the kitchen and its condition. That was a shocking sight for me as I had never lived in such pathetic conditions. Despite it all and to be fair, the girls were kind-hearted. I can say that they did their absolute best to make me feel comfortable and welcome.

I think the only good thing about the accommodation was that it was just a walking distance to the workplace.

Every morning, I had to gather with the rest of the purchasers in front of the office and wait for the bus that would take us to the market. From there we used to make our way walking to the shops.

The sun was at its hottest during that time. At times it felt as though I was melting out of its intensity.

I believe everybody knows that summer is unbearable in the UAE. Disregarding the humidity, mugginess, and stickiness, I was strolling the tiring streets of Deira Gold Souk, and Dragon markets. I was dealing and working with suppliers. After that, I was spending the rest of the day in the hypermarket looking after the section and its displays.

Even though my Urdu was unaccustomed and my English got broken, I managed to do the job.

Maybe attending weekly meetings and giving explanations on the sales was the only thing I enjoyed and found it aligned with my core values.

It was the only task I desired to do.

For a moment, let's just ignore the fact that the job was not to my liking. But what made it worse was I didn't feel welcome. I felt like an outsider and no one really accepted me except for a few.

"She is young and this job is not for her. She is coming to waste our time." The behavior and hard time given would say it all. They did their absolute best to kick me out and yes they succeeded (because I allowed it all to affect me).

I felt like I was being picked on more than the others and accused of being the new girl.

I would cry almost every night on how my life had come to. I was so bothered by the stress and uneasiness of still being lost. It wasn't my cup of tea. That wasn't me or what I wanted.

The people, the job, the aura. I knew that the journey would never be easy, but everything made me feel like a stranger. The increment that I was promised didn't happen and so I decided to leave. I couldn't bear it anymore.

War II: Rejection Is a Redirection

Quitting the job meant quitting the accommodation too. To put it in another way, I became jobless and homeless at the same time. Earlier, I didn't know what it felt like to be so. But when it happened, it was excruciatingly hard, I have to confess.

I managed to stay at my sister's friend's house, but not for long. I had to keep looking for another job and shelter. I had to rely on myself, and not be a burden on someone else.

I concluded that for me to get what I came for, I had to choose to leave depression and procrastination and forge a new set of plans that would lead me to my dream job. So, I printed out many copies of my CV and went distributing them to the retail stores of different malls. It didn't occur to me that I couldn't do that, and so I did it without any hesitation.

I was blessed to receive a call very soon, inviting me for an interview with one of the fashion stores.

I took it seriously and got myself perfectly ready. From the questions to the business attire and makeup.

And yes, I earned the job and signed the offer letter. Alas, joining wasn't immediate as the employment visa would take a while. And that "while" meant months.

Around the same time, I applied for one of the airlines and finally got the assessment day invitation. The opportunity I believed blindly would leapfrog my way to success.

With so much change, I felt my confidence regenerating. I felt life was smiling back at me again and giving me a glimmer of hope.

Thinking and planning, I managed to find another room for four people in another emirate. It was clean and close in a way to the new workplace as well as to the busiest airport in UAE.

I managed to convince the owner to take it the way it was because I wanted to move as soon as possible and felt (always remember that you're feeling your thinking) that I had become a burden on my friend, especially after borrowing from her some money to get the new flat. I promised to give it back on receiving the first salary and left.

I was the first tenant. This time there was neither a fridge nor cooker or internet. But at least, there was new furniture and most importantly a proper bed to sleep on.

This time I had to live again in difficult conditions, but differently. I wasn't able to cook and managed to live on canned food.

To kill time, I went every day to a nearby mall to spend some time and get a free Wi-Fi connection.

There were days when I was able to buy a coffee and days when I couldn't. I knew that I was running out of money and no one else was left to provide me with it. I knew that I had to shut my eyes to the expensive shops.

There were other days when I compelled myself just to sit on the balcony to minimize the cost and drink a cup of tea I made myself, listen to the same list of music and just look dreamily at the airplanes taking off and landing.

I felt so poor, yet so rich in determination. I was and still am hungry for growth. I harbored an ambition and it was taking me so long. It was emptying my tank of patience.

The only hope that kept me motivated in all of that was the assessment day that would happen within a month.

Yet, here was another trouble stressing me out. I realized that I didn't have sufficient money to go all the way to the other emirate for the interview. To go and ask my sister's friend again for money was a blocked way for me. It was very embarrassing and I would come across as needy.

To rewind a bit: Some days before that, I was rolling my trolley in one of the supermarkets. I happened to see a guy talking to two girls who appeared like cabin crew. I don't know if this sounds biased to judge and classify people's occupations as per their appearance, but a small voice whispered and told me that they were. My eyes lit up and my gut felt moved.

I knew that walking in a straight line would not get me far. I had to force myself and practice randomness and take the action of talking to strangers in the most unlikely way. So, I initiated a conversation with him when both of them left and eventually, my instinct didn't lie. They were both working in aviation and he was in retail.

It happened that we met later on and remained in contact. I talked to him about my passion and interest, the challenges I was facing, and the problems I was trying to solve as he did. And we ended up close friends. He was the one who lent me a decent amount of money even in his deepest financial crisis.

See, if I had not broken the ice and approached him, I would not have been able to manage the money and go for the interview. I would not have been able to gain him as a friend.

[Hamza, if you're reading this right here, know that my

gratitude will always go to you. Your support and guidance since the very beginning is priceless. I know that I ate your brain so many times repeating my vision over and over again. Thanks for being a trusted friend and a good listener. Thanks a million.]

[You can notice that my debts were arising and I hadn't even started working.]

Coming back to my assessment day. While I was doing my calculations, I found that the amount wasn't enough for me to have a two-way trip by taxi and keep some for my grocery shopping. So, I had to use the cheapest transport. The bus was the only way.

And that was another problem because I had no idea about the times. The key was to implement randomness again and ask people from all edges. Eventually, they guided me to the main bus station from which I confirmed the correct schedule.

Back to my life in the new house, the days passed and the broker started bringing in new tenants. No more privacy, but I looked at the positive angle of it. There would be some human connection. The girls were Arabic and humble. We were comfortable being roommates, talking to and hanging out with each other from time to time.

The interview date was getting closer, so I had to start my preparations. I needed to focus. You can imagine how that step could change my entire life.

Of course, I couldn't revise in my room either in the morning or at night. In the morning, the girls would be asleep, so disturbing was prohibited. At night, they would be watching TV and chilling around. I needed space and privacy to reflect, analyze, and anticipate. I needed stillness to get ready for a life's performance. For a dream that had kept me suffering for so long.

Here's what I did, I took the sheets of paper I crossed seas with and sat in the family park facing our residence. It was eight in the morning when I started rehearsing.

I was talking to myself and cared about nobody around. I practiced as much as I could and ensured that I covered all that was needed to be a competitive candidate.

I printed the CV and kept all the required documents in a neat and clean folder, and came back home.

Amazingly, everything was ready ahead of time.

That night I couldn't sleep. It wasn't just a matter of adrenaline stimulation. I wish it was. But the reason was different. The girls fought, and their shouting filled up the whole flat if not the entire residence. What a horrible night it was!

Thanks to them for taking away the bit of sleep I was craving to have.

Anyhow, I managed to close my eyes, but my mind was fully awake. It was counting the minutes left for the alarm to ring at three a.m.

It was useless to torture myself, so I stood up and enjoyed the privacy in the bathroom I had to get ready and look as presentable and polished as possible.

I had to take a taxi to the central bus station and from there catch the bus departing at five in the morning.

It was six forty-five when I reached the closest bus stop, and from there again, I had to take another taxi to get me to the training center. I made it and was there at seven thirty to find all the candidates queuing.

You could see everyone in their business attire and showing their invitation at the gate.

I was confident and perfectly set.

Everything went well, I was passing from one stage to another. And every step was getting me closer to my dream.

In my conversation with the recruiter during the last stage, I was asked if I was honest with my age when I applied online. My heart clinked and my brain sounded out a warning bell on that question.

"Yes, I was," I answered.

We carried on with the final questions and pretended like I heard nothing, but this was unexpected "You should reapply after turning twenty-one," said the recruiter.

I couldn't help it. My hopes were dashed. I went home that day, feeling deflated.

I remember myself sitting in the park crying, feeling lonely and devastated. Filled with unsurpassed zeal that had been crushed, I wanted to take out all the frustration and sadness inside me.

By getting doors slammed in my face, I felt weak. I was wallowing in self-pity and disappointment.

I felt that I had slogged my guts out, did my best, gave my all, sold my grannies, and sweated blood. Yet, nothing was going right.

I will never forget that day. It made me emotional and broke me wide. It hit me right in the heart.

War III: The New Direction

Thankfully, within two days, I received a call from my new employer. The employment visa was finally ready and that allowed me to start working.

This made me get out of my depression and re-focus on my goals.

I needed to hold my doubts back and be grateful. Thus, I kept my dream close to my chest and adopted the appearance of dedication, commitment, reliability, diligence, and stability to the new occupation.

This workplace was far better than the previous one. It was and is still famous in the retail competitive marketplace.

The first day, I couldn't feel my feet. Standing for long hours, running from one section to another looking for sizes, and learning how to steam (unfortunately, it's still something I can't do properly).

I also found out that I didn't only have to know the brands in my section which was for women, but for the other sections too: kids, men, and housing. I found myself responsible as the rest for rectifying the small matters of customers while finding it tough to mingle and recall the different brands and procedures.

If you ever worked as a sales consultant, you would know what I am talking about.

By the way, I always take the time to greet every sales associate and give them plenty of recognition because I was in their shoes once and I know what it feels like standing on your feet for long hours. I deeply understand that feeling when you enter a fitting room and find tons of clothes thrown for you on the floor to collect.

One manager read me correctly. His name was Majdi. I got the proper direction from him. He was the only one who could see my future occupation. "Remember this. One day you would have that job where you can be off for three days a week and see the world." He had that talent-spotting skills. He didn't see a failure. On the contrary, he saw a future board member. He didn't keep me short and knew how to motivate me when I was demotivated.

Working in Dubai Mall, one of the largest malls in the world, and knowing what fashion is about were good opportunities for me. I felt blessed.

It was such fun meeting different people and learning about various brands like Marchesa, Rami Al Ali, Zeena Zaki, Valentino, Pinko Carolina Herrera, Karl Lagerfeld, and much more.

It was a pleasure meeting celebrities and conducting events.

The days and weeks passed until I started feeling more confident and comfortable with the job.

Here I would love to take a moment and salute all my colleagues and especially Ameed for his great assistance as a manager too and so many others. You were all splendid and supportive.

Thursday meetings were dull for most of the stuff, but for me, they were the best. It was the day of the week when we used to gather and display the new arrivals.

It was my favorite task to describe every detail of the item. You would find me preparing and studying as if I would give the performance of my life.

I love public speaking. I find it a powerful and uneasy thing to master.

One day I was put in a spot by one of my colleagues who worked for Elizabeth Franchi. She got me a white dress from the new collection and begged me to present it.

"But I am not prepared. I have no idea about the story behind it or even what texture it is made of," I said.

"Come on, you have a thrilling confidence and can talk in front of anyone. Just think about one to two sentences and narrate them in your lovely style," she insisted.

I couldn't say no and found myself flipping quickly through the brand's official page.

I had but five minutes to gather my thoughts and create a

script that would grab everyone's attention.

The meeting was over and I found Majdi coming and congratulating me again on the good script. His appreciation flipped me over with happiness and got me to spend my day eagerly.

[If you are a leader or manager here, please always remember to appreciate your team. It does bring seeds to their deeds.]

War IV: "I Can't Fake It Anymore"

Until then, I thought life would become a little flexible and subtle with me, but it didn't.

The mall was quite far from my home. Taking the metro was not an option as the link was too far away. Ending it was a grueling journey by itself. That time was added to the eight hours of standing at work which I had to take into account.

The second thing was related to its working hours. They were not matching with my work schedule.

There was only one solution: people guided me to a nearby area from where I could get a shuttle to the mall.

To catch that bus, one had to walk for thirty to forty minutes and cross a bridge. My way was made from Deira City Centre every day to both streets of Muraqabat and Rigga.

That meant waking up two hours ahead of the check-in time and reaching home late at night. A few hours of sleep and the same cycle was repeated the next day again.

I had no choice. There were days when I couldn't catch the shuttle even after walking all that distance and ended up taking a taxi and paying the high fares.

On top of that, I was still managing to cook at home and take my meals with me to work.

"Bring it on" was my attitude. Three months doesn't sound

like a long time, but it felt like infinity. It felt like hard labor by itself. And resisting upheavals was futile. To remain patient was the only card I had. So often, I was pushing myself to look at the bright side: having a job, being surrounded by good people, and having an income to pay my bills and debts.

But two more things were making me uncomfortable: the house and transport. Finding my comfort meant giving half of my salary for rent. Again, I had to sacrifice and shift to live near the shuttle area itself.

Whenever I think of the moment I had to get that luggage shifted with me in the taxis and metros, and the number of times I had to rearrange everything, I feel tired.

Getting done with shifting, I started to feel demotivated at work. It was like an endless war. I felt that my journey was taking me from one climax to another.

That thought of "I am not living my passion" started torturing me again. It got activated every time a colleague of mine told me "You look like a flight attendant. Why don't you apply for it? You have what it takes so don't waste your time."

Such simple advice filled with both: hope and sadness. They didn't know that was the thing I had crossed the seas and left the comfort of my own home for.

No one knew what was going on inside my head. No one knew what lofty heights I aspired to.

There is this saying: "Walk a mile in someone's shoes, they say, and chances are you'll be a mile away: but you've got their shoes, make a run for it."

You can be productive, effective, industrious, sober, reliable, and responsible. But not happy. It's actually about what goes on in the background. That was my case.

I was in a good job, in a big fashion department store, and in the most successful mall in the whole world. It wasn't easy but it wasn't hard either. Showing up, contributing, being flexible and adapting to different work schedules, working with colleagues, dealing with the challenges, and then going home all the way walking. I couldn't say no to the ongoing learning experience this time and quit as I did with the previous job.

I was one of the very best. But I wasn't living my Dharma (my calling). I realized that I wasn't growing as I wanted. I felt restricted. I felt chained. The role didn't fill my shoes and satisfy my soul. And as I have a very transparent face, it all started showing.

Here's my point; If you are not passionate about your work, what are you going to be passionate about? [That's the main idea of my first book *Cabin Crew – The Luminaries*.]

Yes, I was making good money to pay my bills and financially it didn't make sense to leave. But spiritually and mentally, it did because I believe in this: if you see your job as a vehicle to pay your bills, then you're not in the right place. You've got to find your true passion. I felt the same feelings every day and still every morning I had to wake up and put that uniform on to get back to the daily routine.

There, I couldn't help myself because it was a matter of age for me, not a skill to fine-tune. I had but to wait. Somewhere, I knew that the delays were happening for a reason.

I didn't give up on trying and spent most of my off days and rest periods filling up applications with different airlines. I didn't have a laptop back then so I had to pay the typing centers per hour. There was one very close to my previous house. I bet the staff knew me by name as the time I spent there was more than the time spent in my room.

"Once you become closer to the required age, we will be able to contact you." This was the only email coming from most of the applications I submitted.

The Mission Kicked Off

The rough times had to pass and the clouds had to be cleared to bring in the illumination: One night, I was in bed and an opportunity lurked that had my eyes glowing fairly and my hope rekindling. It had me bubbling over with enthusiasm: an open cabin crew vacancy, requiring the very young age I came with.

Ultimately, the promising day happened and allowed me to do the very best I could to make it through successfully and reap the fruits of sustained discipline, dedication, and practice.

To get the golden call, I had to wait for two months. I swear that it felt more like two years. I felt every second, every minute, and every hour. Only I know how it was.

It may seem surprising to say that struggles still kept on coming at me from all directions even after resigning and attaining my dream job. I found myself in a deep financial crisis. Shifting again from one emirate to another wasn't as easy as it sounds. I remember during my initial cabin crew training not having a permanent shelter. I was somewhere and my luggage was somewhere else. I vividly remember spending sleepless nights revising for my exams and also fighting with my weight gain again.

The ride was scary, but gratifying.

The Momentum

I am here alive and here's a nugget of advice: If you are passionate about what you do then standing up for it isn't that hard. That's how I felt. That's how I knew that being passionate means caring about what you do. That's how I understood the real meaning of passion which is an alternative to suffering in the Latin root.

When COVID-19 covered the whole world, I knew my work choice wasn't random. That it was real and wise enough. The significance of having an intrinsic motivation.

That's the importance of knowing your drive and finding what truly makes you tick, what's your life purpose and the reason for your being. It's the higher urge to clarify and crystal-clear your "why" and to always pick that path with your heart.

I find that much of my job relies on time management, communication, teamwork, and customer service skills. All those benefits I have gained along the way through my previous job. I didn't know then that God was preparing me for what I wanted. He wanted me to become better.

Climbing for passion, not glory or money has always been my mantra.

For me, reaching a high level of knowledge in my job will forever be my number one mission. Something that I won't compromise with.

Remember this: Every job is noble even if it's not spiritually fulfilling.

My journey in aviation itself is still full of ups and downs. And that's simply fighting for our purpose.

[I want to address everybody who asked me why I am so mature compared to my age and why I am so determined when it comes to my dreams. I hope this certain phase of my race has answered your questions.]

I could not have thought that I would find myself in amazing roles.

All of which forced me to become stronger, and sharper in ways I could not have imagined.

My story and I believe some of yours can back this up: "A smooth sea never made a skilled sailor."

So, do the hard things first.

Chapter 4

Discipline Is Earned

"Discipline is the bridge between goals and accomplishments."
— Jim Rohn

"I can't do this anymore." I cried on the chemical burn of the eyelash glue as I struggled to zip my back dress up.

"God!" I screamed.

On the 2nd of July 2022. I had to go and shoot for my cover book *Cabin Crew – The Luminaries*.

It was crazy and super-hot then. What a horrendous and hovering condition: half my makeup wasn't done with no idea of how the hell I would wear the scarf or the hat I had bought.

Doubts were casting a shadow upon me. One more wrong thought and a work of years would collapse.

Years of sacrifice and sincere effort; purchasing books, learning how to become a speed reader (and so becoming one), understanding the art of writing, and putting in the hour every day obsessively and tirelessly.

Years of building a new Nawres in a new arena.

Finding a suitable cover was a roller-coaster by itself. I had enough before this photoshoot of clicking pictures.

Turning my thinking around, I found the idea of giving up would be crushing. I had to finish what I started. Discipline sometimes is all that you have. It helps you progress even when all seems lost.

With the clock ticking and the photographer reaching my building, I was obliged to end the mess I was in any way.

Rebooted, I took my accessories and makeup kit in hand and wore my heels.

Wondering about my dress? Never mind. It was sorted out.

I puffed away a sigh of relief when I found a woman in the lift to close it for me. "You saved my life," I said, sending her good blessings out there in the air.

I am sure she was wondering why I was in such a rush.

Anyhow, it was God's fate and proper timing.

The backstory of my *Cabin Crew – The Luminaries* book began in March 2020, during those early days of COVID-19.

There was a fire in my belly to handcraft it. I thought of the tough journey I had gone through to deliver such ambition back in the day. I felt I could use my experience and hard-earned lessons as wisdom and inspiration for the future cabin crew. That I could ultimately share my passion for soaring, serving, and writing.

As I have told you, I didn't have the privilege to pay for the aviation course. I struggled to ask people from all the edges. I urgently needed one book that could guide me until the end so I created one.

I thought mostly of those unfamiliar with the role, not knowing where to start, having tons of questions about the hiring process, and not being able to afford the studies or courses.

I wanted to prove that we do not need a lot of money to reach our goals as much as we need good knowledge and deliberate practice.

To inspire them to do the things that inspire them, so that together we build a world of luminaries.

So effective that it's coming these days with tremendous changes: it's creating significant changes for the readers.

Something even bigger got me striving for the read. There is this bigger picture I wanted them to see:

The field needs more passionate people. And it's a great feeling to do the job wholeheartedly and lead it with unbeatable interest, vision for greatness, deliberation, and consideration.

Tragically, the pandemic affected the aviation industry and made the cabin crew dream for thousands if not masses seem out of reach.

I didn't want them to lose faith. I saw the guide as a motivator so they can today choose the dead time to be alive.

I insisted on proving that all we need is a positive mindset for long-term success.

Not everyone shared my passion at work and that made the vision surrounded by dream attackers.

Nims Purja's saying emphasizes the same point, "In life, you have to keep doing what you believe. You have to keep asking yourself. Do you want this from your heart? Is it for self-glory? Or is it something bigger? Sometimes the ideas you come up with may seem impossible to the rest of the world, but that doesn't mean it's impossible to you."

Would it take off and reach the readership? I couldn't tell, but I had to know for sure that I was heading in the right direction. "Just wait and see. I mean it," I murmured to myself as I continued to stay loyal to my gut as must you.

All this was good and well but still, I had to work more and more on materializing the idea and making it come to pass.

An author needs to have good writing skills. It's obviously the most basic foundation needed and mine was not that fully formed.

My lack of experience could previously be regarded as an equally minor setback, but with time and endeavor, I was able to put it behind me. I worked bloody hard to bombproof such an aptitude.

As the flight operations started increasing, I had to mission-plan my schedule of scripting and importantly balance between two of my life aspects, work, and personal growth.

The morning routine I adopted then played perfectly in my sphere. During the uneasy times when you think there can't be a handle or keyhole, you find the early morning rise swings open at your touch. Jumping and drop-kicking into so much, cutting in the never-ending preoccupations. Honest.

Ever since it has been a long and good time being an early morning bird and learning about the flow state science. The analogy of doing that caused me to be more of a disciplined person. Saying that, I haven't been primed genetically for any will. When I was a kid, my parents used to send me to primary school on my own. They showed me the way once and left me alone for the thirteen years that followed. It's like I was thrown into real-life situations.

They made me work so hard too for whatever I asked them for. But I never got a reward before showing them results. That probably sounds like torture but it wasn't. I needed every scrap of that. I can say my parents did a good job for taking a part in teaching me discipline and I am happy that it has eventually been my number one attitude.

That being said, I wasn't born naturally for such a power. I have taken the required steps.

However, I knew it would still prove to be a tough task regardless of my enthusiasm for the read.

An obstacle appeared and then another. And another. They seemed to grow and I had to knock them down, one by one.

Desiring the book to be more expressive and helpful, I

decided to capture as much as I could of the essence of the book through some artwork.

I looked up, asking God for a good sign and there it came unexpectedly. Finding an illustrator triggered this: the world had my back. A voice of reason and the right dimension.

The payments on the way up for that were horrific. The heavy deductions of early COVID-19 and preoccupations compelled me to squeeze budgets.

Because I was a firm believer in whatever I was doing, I took responsibility. I decided to be on the cause side of life and be fully in control of my outcomes and results in life.

"Cause causes certain effect."
— Robert Simic

It was easy to sulk, but I endured so much in a period when things were not encouraging or easy. In a hellish time marked by angst and insecurities.

When I was well on track to completing my mission, my "half-breakup" happened. For a brief time, I thought it was all over. That I wouldn't be able to carry on. My book was in jeopardy. That was the most pressing and avalanche issue.

I was very human and so stepping on my heart wasn't that easy on me. There were moments when I felt so overwhelmed. The heavy encounter became a dangerous opponent.

Option one was to give up

Option two was to carry on with an inner strife It was the second option that I chose.

I didn't want to tell my small social network that I was going through a vulnerable process that could put me off at any moment.

Dealing with my emotions was the hardest job on the way. My first plan of action was to work hard on controlling my emotions through writing itself. I had to work through both equally. Balance, balance, and nothing but balance.

I remember there were times when I would write for five to six hours and then go unleashing my pain temporarily in walking, dancing, a friendly chit-chat, and even sometimes crying, so I could manage my focus and flow state for the following day.

The winds of sadness enjoyed whipping me up, but I chose again to acknowledge it and I can say that my discipline was my escape rope, my protector, and my trustworthy backup as in any other never-ending battle.

The traumatic encounter left some mental scars. I was annoyed with myself. I was sick and tired of the memories that kept torturing me whenever I sat down at my desk.

Dusting myself down and getting back in the game was the only option. It was down to me to fix it. Facing it but never running from it.

I worked hard every day to push the story out.

Finally, getting the read approved and signing the contract made me realize that nothing could stop me or smash my discipline that had been built due to being focused, setting a long-term goal, navigating challenging pressure, and pressing ahead peerlessly.

For much of those past three years, I had dealt with a huge expedition.

It was mind-blowing on all the levels. The sound of three years and a half in my mouth feels like a great stone that I want to spit out. I thought for the thousandth time, about how it had got to such a vast amount of time.

Handcrafting *Cabin Crew – The Luminaries* was a hectic excursion that took as much as it gave me.

I wrote it when all I had was a screen-cracked laptop and a four hundred and sixty square feet studio. When I felt like it, and when I didn't. When I became at times weighed down by the words going tough and uneasy to be provoked.

I remember carrying the manuscript with me everywhere I went. I felt it being my baby, my firstborn.

I cannot deny that I also wrote it when I was feeling unbeatable and utterly optimistic.

It was all emotional, challenging, and fascinating. How could one book make you feel this much? The one question that was popping up in my mind so often.

The air changed. I changed. How beautiful writing can be.

Here's the thing:

We often don't feel like doing it. We hate to wake up too early. We don't like getting ready and going to the gym. We don't want to sign up for duty and everyone hates "Mondays." We think of giving up the moment we hit a big fat roadblock. But, so many of us are still able to make it. Why?

Discipline (apart from the strong intention we hold) is the answer. It's the power that fuels you to do it regardless of all the demotivating feelings.

One thing I truly admire about discipline is that it backs you up when motivation disappears.

It gives you the urge to finish what you started. It's like your everyday reminder.

You know, you can't sit around and wait for the right mood to strike.

In return, you tend to stretch your abilities and mighty missions beyond what's fun.

Theodore Roosevelt got it right when he said: "Nothing in the world is worth having or worth doing unless it means effort, pain, difficulty."

With this in mind, what happens is that when we stop taking action, we fall into "Inaction that breeds doubt and fear." In the words of Dale Carnegie, "Action breeds confidence and courage. If you want to conquer fear, do not sit at home and think about it. Go out and get busy."

Slowly, you will start to notice that you're speeding up. That you're making progress. So much of what I do personally is uncomfortable, but, because I'm disciplined, I keep doing it; I remember throwing tons of my writing drafts in the dustbin when I started.

It was not easy putting myself on the track over and over again. Nothing felt right as a beginner.

That wasn't how I thought it would be. I wanted to become the best I could be at writing, speaking, and coaching. That required a system of practice.

Practicing deliberately has made me feel better and even more confident with my writing skills. It has made me disciplined. If you want to fathom the science of how people become so disciplined and obsessed with what they do, practice is the best example to give.

With this in mind, discipline and practice work hand in hand.

Deliberate Practice provides you with the key to quickly becoming disciplined and good at what you do. The term was discovered by Anders Ericsson in the 1990s to describe the style of serious study as the purpose of effectively improving an individual's performance.

It's beyond what's "comfortable," "familiar," and "easy." We truly develop greatness the hard way.

To delve deeper into the practice part, it's not only about locking yourself in a room for hours, it's also about the quality of practice you put in. It's about being focused on the right and important tasks that are meaningful to you, while urgent tasks are often related to someone else's needs. (That's what I guide my clients towards.)

You practice with your all: your soul, heart, mind, and body.

You must give it your best energy.

That's what starts to define the quality of your work as well as the quality of your discipline. The difference between the "ordinary" and the "extraordinary" shows up.

So, it's not just what you do. It's not the natural talent you have either.

It's how disciplined you are. How eager you are to approach your intention and give it the amount of practice it requires.

Here's what I do as well: Every six months, I self-evaluate

myself. I ask myself a lot of questions.

I attend writing conferences and go for retreats as a different way of practicing. I dance with people who are better at dancing so I feel challenged and have the urge to practice even more.

You too, can have a mentor (I'm still having a mentor myself as I continue to be a learner).

I have learned that education from someone else is always important. You can always challenge yourself to become better. You've got to start thinking many doors.

This then explains that discipline is a constant work in progress.

Discipline is like a muscle: you can work it out day after day and month after month. strengthen and nurture it.

That means it's earned. If you know now that discipline is earned and you can build it too, will you make a move?

I ask you again: Will you make a move today?

Needless to say, my first book possesses a very special spot in my heart because it has played a big role in shaping and turning me into the person I am today. It has made me a real fighter, a real warrior that fears none. It has made me a misfit.

I can say it was the breath I had to breathe continuously to survive. The motivation that I woke up for every day. The antidote and vaccination against the early unsettled stages of the epidemic. The intimate friend who knew and felt me better. The mirror I reflected through my true self and hidden talents. The guide that helped me go from being lost and sad to getting my life into shape.

I even felt empty the moment I submitted it because it was fulfilling and gratifying.

I put my heart and soul into it. I gave it my all. The sweat and elbow grease certainly went too.

I'm hoping that the read has injected hope in so many hearts.

The bottom line or the game-changing lesson is this:

Discipline is the virtue that sets our races on fire and makes each one of us strong enough to keep going.

Emerged, it's the athletic guide. The deputy when all forms of motivation disappear.

Baking Your Self-Discipline

First, You Build Discipline, and Then You Own Your Race!

Have an Aim to Wake Up for
No aims, no discipline.

Without an aim, it cannot be activated. If the mind feels unresponsive in life, it cannot do much for us. As you start working towards your goal, your brain will automatically economize.

Choose Distal Goals
Don't go for the immediate reward (short goals) because they're uncompromising and insistent sometimes. Here I illustrate: If we are unable to accomplish what we are supposed to do at this time, we might feel stressed and pressurized. And that is what exhausts us. With sufficient time, we can extend the level of commitment and also guarantee the completion of the target.

Be a goal-oriented person to avoid inner conflicts: Our mental vigor is limited and whenever we are attempting to focus on one thing, we are eliminating our capacities for the rest.

Train like War. Rest like Heaven
Having enough rest: Self-control can be depleted from overuse, as I highlighted earlier. Everything consumes much of our

determination, and for that, we feel anxious most of the time. Resting it then means empowering it. Remember, a rested will is a stronger will.

Sit alone and do nothing. If you receive a call, don't answer. Just relax and encompass the silence.

Reward Yourself with Glucose

We lose self-control and become closer to temptation and depression. Have your glucose intake from the sluggish-burning food.

Repeat and Practice

Repetition and regular practice. Yeah. Willpower is like a muscle: the harder you train it, the stronger it becomes.

Make Difficult Decisions and Adopt Difficult Behavior

Step out of the comfort harbor and learn from the tough seasons. We cannot grow in a time of ease. I said it somewhere in this read and here we can relate. If our brains are used to mundane and monotonous rituals, the level of self-control cannot expand.

Ensure the rituals are self-control-based like rising with the sunup, cutting off sugar for some time, and so on. Those uncomfortable things require much discipline.

To have an unstoppable discipline, we must reflect and do big. We must go for whatever is uncommon and not inhabited. We must commit to the fall lines and trust the process.

Chapter 5

Tap Into Your Potential to Bombproof It

"We have so much unexpressed potential."
– Oprah Winfrey

Everyone has a thrilling potential. A special talent residing in his soul. A unique aptitude that others can neither have nor understand.

Keeping a full "what it takes" fastened and secured not only harms us but also does a disfavor to others. I believe in this: We were brought into this world to serve and save it in our own way and that's a responsibility to take to the point of no return. I have made it my plan to be in charge.

It's important here to note Swami Rama's saying: "Human birth is not an accidental phenomenon. It has a purpose. A human being is born to accomplish a goal."

Everyone must listen to himself. There must be something whispering to him, guiding him someplace stupendous. Something that he loves doing the most. Something that he finds in a time of ease and discord. Something that sets his soul free and alive.

Having said that, your potential is your "why" and "calling." Your "Dharma" is what gives you the course of action. You become more capable of sustaining your motivation and focus even for the long term.

The potential of writing spoke to me long ago when I was

in high school. We had a big event called English Day meant for the talent and entertainment communities. We were encouraged to participate and unleash those hidden potentials. With a spirit full of enthusiasm, I took part. I had the heart too and felt there could be some gifts and talents to demonstrate.

Some chose guitar and singing and others acting. And I chose writing. Yeah. Writing. I found it so close to me.

The love of literature was there. I realized it. There has always been an unexplained attachment to papers, pens, and publishing life-giving quotes on the social media platform.

So, I wrote an article called "Dear Government" for the chaotic times we were all going through back home after the revolution of January 2011 that affected noticeably our education, employment, and security.

I wanted to encourage the politicians to rise and do something for the public. [Perhaps, I was too young to fathom politics. Whatever.] Ideas emerged and allowed me to construct an interesting message.

We planned for rehearsal, and surprisingly I was requested to be the presenter for our talented team. The teacher saw in me the talent of presenting. "It requires character, confidence, and eloquence. And you have that," she said.

Me? A presenter? Another rush of happiness covered me for getting the scope to do one more thing I love, Public Speaking.

I can say that being a life coach today is not a coincidence.

I was serious about it and started preparing as if I would give a worldwide performance.

I wanted to polish my knowledge of the whole thing. I wanted and needed to be entitled to talent and responsibility. For that, I spent my days researching the most successful tactics for speaking and presenting. I wanted to live the role like a fireball. And I did.

The event room was overflowing with leaflets, decorating tools, and loud hailers. It was well prepared and almost all the teachers and students came over.

Standing on the stage, holding my notes in one hand and microphone in another, whilst facing the mob, made me feel like I belonged there. I sensed something being unleashed and liberated.

My well-paced speech echoed in the hall. The entire audience was looking at me and that was damn scary.

Somehow, I managed to control the stage without fear. And what a sense of achievement for a fifteen-year-old girl. When the crowd stood and broke into applause, something again clicked inside, and the ambition started taking root.

How did I realize that I love public speaking? I would always hold the remote control and pretend that I was on a TV show being hosted to talk about self-improvement and narrate successful people's stories. I would imagine myself representing empowerment in the sense of refusing to give up and believing in the possibilities of change. I don't know if one of you has ever done that too and felt like "What the heck am I doing? Am I a psycho?" Never mind; those are not signs and symptoms of a psychological disorder. That's your spirit (state of being) talking to you.

Truly, how powerful your narrative can be. That story you write for yourself.

I would just watch the news to see how desperately confident and stunning those presenters were. Reading a full script without even blinking an eye.

I would enjoy the time when nobody was home so I could

turn the music louder and just start creating some moves and performing as a dancer and then proceed to my "TV Show hosting time."

I can say that joining the dance community today has some old roots and habits. As you can see, nothing is coincidental.

The same Celine Dion' songs that I used to listen to when I was nine years old and repeated a zillion times over led me to the path of choosing English instead of Law at college.

Writing and public speaking were stirred in me as a teenager. And as I grew older, they grew bigger with me. I have started adopting them ever since.

When I worked in retail and had to stand for eight complete hours on my feet, I could be seen holding a paper and pen. Morning shifts were the best for me to do that as almost none from the management and staff were around. Everyone loved the night shifts, except me.

Obviously, I couldn't find a better time than the pandemic to bombproof that.

In times of Instagram, Netflix, and big TVs, I won't bother spending my days off just at home reading and learning from those great authors. I would put at least four hours a day into practicing and enriching my jargon. Constant small steps without distractions.

Tell me a word or an idea and I will write an article if not a book about it.

Up until today, I truly consider writing a lifetime preoccupation that I have to give sufficient time and care to. It's the world that I feel lost without. I would go mad if I didn't get one hour at least for myself; doing what I see as more important than anything else.

Becoming an author sounded like an insane dream of

fantasy at first, but there were so many reasons and omens. Then I knew that my Deity placed them on my way for a reason. I saw signs, big fingers coming up from heaven.

I was secretly longing to become an artist. I had to beat the myths and go for something my family didn't like or want to approve. It was like a never-ending war.

They wanted me to become the next "lawyer" or "judge" of the family, as to become the second version of my sister. To get trapped in "the shadow pursuits" is about the fear of taking it all seriously. They believed in the "perceived security" and I simply didn't want to.

I fought for what I'm truly aligned with.

"Almost every man wastes part of his life in attempts to display qualities which he does not possess."
— Samuel Johnson

Speaking about "speaking," it's natural. But public speaking is a skill for which I have been working on. I won't forget how I felt the first time I started training in aviation or the first time I coached my clients. I felt myself flying.

And so, here's the thing: never define yourself by what you do, but by why you do it.

I always get this question, "What motivates you?"

It's simply my "WHY." It's for what I am here today, to do and accomplish through those potentials.

I'm well aware that I have a profound calling. My mission is to make myself a growth-conscious individual.

Today, I have the titles of author, coach, and speaker. But I am not my titles. I am the value those occupations make the spiritual heart feel. Because I am a WOA (Work of Art) a beautiful term created by Ajit Nawalkha, the life coach. I continue to learn, dream, and grow those potentials.

I am buzzing with excitement at the potential of what's within my reach.

I cannot perceive what the future holds for me, but I ensure and promise myself this:

I won't be afraid of hardships. I won't be afraid of failure. I won't be afraid of being wrong. I am only afraid of not maximizing my potential and true gifts. I am not even sure if I have figured everything out but I ensure growing in different places and feeding those creative capacities I have as I believe a career can be more than one thing.

Because a racer full of potential must not be afraid of setting his abilities free and out to the world. Learn to trust the receiving signs. Hit the dislodging button hard. Just kick-start it and see what you can do and what you cannot…

I was not lucky to find what I love from an earlier stage.

It's just a matter of picking the path with the heart. Your spirit knows the way. So why don't you trust it?

I grew up in an environment that didn't teach me how to find out what I'm good at, and why it's important to do that.

Alas, nowadays people struggle to identify what they are capable of. Ask them to write down what they want, and the list never ends. That's what makes most people miss the spark in the eye.

Look now, if I ask you to go for a buffet, do you have to eat everything? Do you have to eat what your mother or brother are eating?

Here's the answer, No, you don't have to.

If you're going to eat everything or do what those around you are doing, then you're still on the lookout.

When you choose what you love, your plate (your soul) becomes full.

The issue here is about what needs to be tried and penetrated inward. You need to keep trying so you figure out the WHY and clear the HOW. I am telling you this because you might still be on the lookout but never really know what it is you're looking for.

You may be thinking "How the hell can I find my true calling and pursue it if I feel I am good at nothing?"

Grabbing that hairbrush, jumping on the sofa and pretending to be a singer performing on the stage, or having a pen in hands with a stethoscope playing to be a doctor.

I believe we all did that. We all dreamt we could be something when we were kids: my dream was to become an anatomist. I don't know why I chose that occupation in my imagination at the age of eight if you would ask me. The thing I know is I was never scared of dead bodies and blood even in those horror movies I loved watching alone when everybody else went to sleep.

What I have observed is this: dreams come to us in all shapes and sizes, and your passion sometimes starts from a place you don't want. From a place you've never thought of. And most importantly it's not something you grew up already knowing but discovering when you fully zone out.

And that's a race in itself by the way: finding out what you're truly good at.

So, if that's where you are right now, take my words into account please:

This might be very difficult for you, but I want you to forget that it's hard because it's just a start. You've got to begin the hunt: try as many things as you can until you get that buzzing sound warning you to stop. Your gut feeling is your GPS out there. [The true potentials are gut-driven and wrenching, that's why they are meant to fill us up spiritually.] It gives us energy.

You will simply know that it's the right thing for you. It will keep rolling in your mind over and over again. It will take most of your time and when you're not doing it, you'll be thinking about it. It will give you that sense of divine jubilation and gratification. There will be a consistent version of you, refusing to start what it can't finish. That somehow this is the thing you were born for and meant to be. It's something you can't honestly define but only feel in your heart.

And again, if you are on the right path there will be certain people and omens especially placed for you.

Because it is a crime to keep that gift locked and buried.

What a waste doing something (for the wrong reasons) that's not aligned with your truth! What a guilt to not to die empty of your gifts…

The potential you have within you will speak to you now or later. I humbly advise you to take your time before you find out what you want to be for the rest of your life and as a suggestion, you can be more than one thing. You can have more than one potential. For that, you've got to dig deeper and deeper. You don't have to limit yourself to one sounding board. You are a racer, so run without limits.

Finding Your WHY

Give this challenge the time it deserves. Use a journal to write down your answers.
(I encourage writing as it slows your thinking.)

1. What activities speak to me?
2. What keeps me alive?
3. Where is my focus going?
4. What has made me believe in that question?
5. What's the main intention behind my driving question?
6. Will it affect me negatively in case I don't achieve it?
7. How would I feel? What would I do?
8. Is it stimulating positive feelings?
9. Any doubts?
10. Is it supporting me on all the levels?
11. What potential do you see in me? (Ask a friend)
12. What do you think are the three strengths that you would call me for when you need help? (Ask a friend)

Chapter 6

"Solitude Is the DNA of Artistry"

"That's dissociation. It's healthy, healing, and productive."
  − Bruce D. Perry

"Ugh, I want to be alone," I scream. A mental pressure is looming over me.

I haven't sat with myself for the past three weeks. And it feels heavy.

It's prompting my frustration. I am starting to feel on edge as my busy life is taking a swing at my face.

That being said, Nawres is out of control and missing herself. Destructions are ubiquitous, so where do I go now?

I have to face the cold truth that as of now I can't do that.

Accepting the current situation is what I'm willing to take.

I'm trying to convince myself there's a way out sooner or later. As the days turn into weeks and the weeks into months, you lose yourself in the crowd. And that's what I hate the most. Just like I've always been. That girl who admires reflecting, traveling, putting her headphones on, and increasing the volume all out whilst listening to her favorite electronic music. [Even while writing this chapter, I am doing so.] All in solitude.

Dreaming, planning, learning, resting, and unbridling potential. Isolated without disruption.

I have a hypothetical world in my mind that's always

speaking loudly. Turning its volume down is speculative and toxic for me.

When I'm alone, I can always calm my busy mind, put things into their right places, and reach my intuition. I start to believe and fathom my difficulties. I get my next strides clear and regain my grounded approach. Life starts to feel better. I find it a helpful way to stay connected to myself.

At some level, you must have some privacy. Your deepest thoughts, most sincere emotions, and gut-driven decisions are coming from those moments of discretion. You can dip in and dip out the untriggered, heal the unhealed, speak the unspeakable, and express the unexpressed.

Identifying it all is winning it all.

The truth is you're not egoistic because do you know what's selfishness? Talking to others and silencing yourself. Giving more time to people and less time to yourself.

And do you know what's scary? Those unresolved and put-off self-conversations lead to complications. Whenever we experience a blockage, our nervous system becomes dysregulated. We start to feel distraught like a failure. A hyperarousal state can befall; antagonism, ADHD, and destructive behavior are the indicating symptoms.

In a word, we tend to navigate a chaotic inner journey.

You may not realize it but all those repressed and unclean inner luggage will pop up again and even harder.

And in most cases, the brain's ability to focus and take in information goes undeveloped.

Your dissociation is not a negative behavior (in case you've been told). Nothing is wrong with a withdrawn person. It's a form of unlocking more self-potential, breeding more self-love, and wiring in more self-respect. It's a form of healing, growing and exalting.

Solitude is your invigorating and enlivening home, your

safe place. It's where dreams and sparks of light happen. And for the most part, it's an art to be mastered.

It's not surprising to recognize that being bombarded and socializing a lot gets you in times lost and fatigued. That it gets you out of your true line. Somehow, you grab a lot of dust and stop knowing what you want: as you hear gossip from here and illusions from there.

The world goes miserable so often. Lily Singh puts it this way: "We go out into the world, we're introduced to an infinite number of things that can distract us. We often forget that we need to clear our minds of all the noise."

Digital devices are the main source of such interruption and destruction nowadays; the emails and notifications you receive, the applications you surf, and the videos you watch. Unfortunately, it is the first thing most people do when they wake up in the morning. It seems easy to move your mind with such interruptions when you are stopping it.

And it is not just that such interruptions affect our cognitive bandwidth, it's also that they breed cortisol in our bloodstreams, the stressful hormone that affects the hippocampus that's also responsible for hoarding stressful experiences.

Once such nerve-racking feelings are stored in the brain, you cannot dismiss them as **the brain wants you to know that you were scared that time you saw a snake – but it doesn't want you to relive the anxiety of the moment.** All of this in return, drains your mental power and ravages your state and output.

If you fail to step out and say no to all the digital noise to protect a work that matters, you'll suffer from disappointment and guilt.

All offense aside, I am not forcing you to live in a bubble

for the rest of your lives. We are social creatures and species. We must mingle. But I have no doubts that isolation is solace and an antidote against all that is poisonous and trivial. I have seen it changing lives including mine.

I believe in its power to clean that dirt you gather and might get suffocated from.

I believe it can help you better understand and hear your inner voice that never lies [keep this in mind: your gut feeling is as pure as your isolation. It's a fact].

I believe it is a scope of discovering your talents and aligning your soul with your core values. I believe it clears your most wanted visions and upcoming moves. I believe it enhances your self-confidence, reliance, and devotion. I believe it heals your wounds and resolves your inner strife. I believe it gives you the room to produce masterpieces. I believe it rejoices you and brings into your mind incredible ideas. I believe it will help you step out into the world stronger, brighter, and wiser.

You may identify yourself in this: Don't call me crazy, but I vividly remember locking myself home for nearly a week without seeing, calling, or texting anybody. With oodles of missed calls, unread work emails, and personal messages, I felt relieved. I tended to declutter messy thoughts and experienced beautiful as well as deep-rooted inner conversations.

Organizing your ideas is like cleaning your messy work desk of all papers, folders, pens, and unnecessary garbage.

I often can't wait for that day off to grab my daily journal and record what it feels like to talk, unpack, analyze, and assess. I give my brain the chance to work through negativity and help me feel safer.

At first, I thought it's a state of a downturn and so many people will try to convince you or maybe have already done that it's one of such. You may very well be running from inner discords.

People will call you crazy for not having a partner, partying hard every night, or posting your everyday life on the social media platform. Calling you crazy for dissociating won't make a big difference either.

We are different: some of us are internal processors while the rest of us are external processors.

My highest inspirational moments and artistic productions are a direct reflection of a clean mental state.

"Creativity requires healthy, well-defined boundaries." Got it right, Todd Henry.

Having said that, artistry happens when you're at peace with yourself and that provokes in return what we call in neuroscience the flow state. It's when you likely can daydream and allow your mind to wonder. It's when you're deeply focused on one task without interruptions.

Just like the Dutch artist Van Gogh when he left his occupation at the Hague branch of an international art dealing firm, to go follow his passion for painting.

The deeper his fervor got, the braver he became to turn off the objective world and open the door to the inner one dwelling inside his head. That world for all is unusual and weird but also artful and magical.

Leaving others most of the time to sit alone and just unleash one idea after the other which but the paper can comprehend... To take off that nagging urge in his brain and create masterpieces until there was no more to create.

And then goes feeling so self-fulfilled, momentous, and enormous even in his deepest sadness whilst seeing his superb creations. Allowing himself to step out into the external world again with masterpieces such as the Sunflower Series, the Potato Eaters, and Self Portrait. The preciousness that the world is still now celebrating and cherishing.

In that mode of isolation, everyone thought he was a mad social running from life when he was indeed running towards it.

"Motivation and flow need to work together, and they must be completed with a solid recovery protocol, like good sleep and nutrition."

— Jim Kwik

If you turn the mirror now and ask yourself from where all those great achievements and wise decisions you've ever made are coming from, you might be able to connect to this: Codifying beautiful and bountiful creations requires quietude and stillness. Think of all the times you sat alone and were able to bring a new method to increase your income, or simply come to a conclusion that you deserve better as you've been stuck in a rut for so long and feeling cynical.

It's a core fact that flow state is a main factor in someone's level of inspiration and productivity. It's conceived when no one else is around.

One must sit alone to find himself and thus his identifiable race.

Chapter 7

Trauma... That Emotional Thunderstorm

"When you experience the world through the lens of trauma, it's easy to miss the opportunity for positive experiences."

— Vex King

Oh, trauma... the pain that can hit you suddenly and place a severe strange weight on your limbs...

One that gets you feeling horrible and devastates all those beautiful thoughts and bits of confidence you possess...

And then it happens to spoil your inner peace and gratification and turn you into a magnet of pessimism at a time when the world is supposed to be full of unsurpassed possibilities.

It gets you uncomfortable, hopeless, and desperate.

In a word, it is a repellent emotional thunderstorm that no one desires to be placed in...

I've got my own pain file that took me almost three years to pull off. It was a one-off experience that got me off track.

On a galactic scale, the trauma I faced a couple of years ago happened to be silent because of a breakup or allow me to say "half-break-up."

It was a one-sided love experience, a good friendship rapport, funded with a lot of desire and based on a deep connection. It was mysterious and adorable, but also complicated. I found the person to be simple, benevolent, and strange in a good sense. I think Chetan Bhagat is right when he wrote: "Sometimes it's hard to explain why you find a person beautiful."

He used to be secretive. Ordinarily, he wouldn't spare so many words but there was always that care in his eyes and voice. He used to read me in great and I loved how he could explore and see within me potential no one else got to see. It was magical how he could sense what I wanted and envisioned even before I thought of it. I felt so comfortable and authentic with him, and I believe he did the same THEN. The two of us were in sync and we ended up reacting in the same beats in so many things. We were close [I perceived].

Scratch that and make the long story short, the relationship did not own a label. I confess… Neither I nor he wanted to be accountable for an official one because we believed in no future gathering us. We saw the world differently.

But there deep inside me, things were going serious and official. I did not realize that I loved him to the point of no return… I kept the feelings to myself and that made my love tough. And I wouldn't have it get that far if I had to… I thought nothing and trusted the flow until he decided to be with someone else later. "Well, I like her," he said icily and with resigned interest.

That hit me like thunder.

Reading that message, I stood near the window numb, figuring out where to go next. It was like a giant "Game- Over" that smashed my entire being. My heart was leaping from my chest.

I was at a loss and all I could say was "wish you all the best" because I had no right to ask for it.

It truly hurts when your favorite person finds another favorite person.

November, fifteenth (I won't mention the year) was a sad

day. It broke me wide open. It got me into an emotional black hole.

He gave me his back and left.

From then on, trauma hit me hard. Deep pain. A slaughtering one. And no one noticed a thing in times when it could be very visible! I found myself struggling and fighting against an unbearable emotional fatigue that left my heart not so strong and the lungs not so elastic... I was hit by a flood of grief. It felt like the death of a beloved one.

His decision made me feel like I was a 'left behind' and got me trapped in a dumb mess. A very critical period of my lifetime that I could only title with "What happened to me?".

Everywhere I went, I saw the scenario reinforced.

I don't know if my story seems to be familiar or normal and if I was a novice or not. I don't know what your perspective is. But one thing I know. I died every day. It wasn't easy on me. I abundantly experienced Russell Brand' saying, "I couldn't cope with being me."

There was that huge internal storm and I had to learn how to survive by myself and for myself. SURVIVAL was my daily lesson.

My post-traumatic stress disorder (PTSD) proved I was foolish for him.

"Psychological trauma is not visible on the outside, and such wounds do not easily heal."

– Toshikazu Kawaguchi

Jealousy

"She has him." That thought itself got me murdered... the feeling condensed into tears and passed through me. It unsettled me a lot. There was a challenging mix of emotions and rational thoughts. It made everything seem and taste bitter.

I would try my best every time not to look at their pictures together and talk myself out of what was sure to be a suicidal sensation of dread and jealousy.

Depression

Worryingly, the "half-breakup" made me feel so outraged and disappointed me a lot. I went into a deep mode of questioning and doubting all the good things he said, the emotions he demonstrated as well as the good time we spent together.

The world had seemed to grow pale, chaotic, and tiresome for me. In real life, we were over. But, for me, we were not... I pictured him everywhere I went, and I found it so difficult to step out and accept the truth that I would not have his presence anymore. There was something silent, forlorn in me. I wanted to forget the world and the dreadful people. I started seeing life through the lens of trauma.

I could not overcome that question of him abandoning me. I lost my way back to love. I couldn't disclose the incident, share my feelings, or pronounce his name to anyone. Even to those I was close to. I felt no one would get me. Restoring and holding it for myself got me depressed and sad for a very long time. I must share: the medicine became the poison and that made me feel worse.

Negative Self-Affirmations and Blame

The incident got me telling myself, "Do you know what? You

are not good enough, she is better than you, you must be missing something, you're scary, boring, or maybe just annoying... You were too much... you should not have gotten involved in such a relationship. You must have not given him the green light."

Loss of Passion
The one thing that scared me the most was this: Being a passionate person, trauma hit those ardent visions I had. It wanted me to stop and get out of my true line. I felt so demotivated and started to doubt my potential and dreams.

Trust Issues
I lost trust in the people around me. My brain had been sending me signals of threat and danger activating my stress response system whenever I tried associating with someone new and that's because all received information from the present moment is compared and influenced by the memories of previous experiences. And I started thinking that everyone would do the same thing: get me attached and then go somewhere. I even lost trust in myself and the choices I would make. Hence that made me adopt a contemptuous behavior I had never wanted to adopt. I did hurt people as I hurt myself, and here I would love to apologize for being so.

That said, I can't help but think of the times I exhausted my mind thinking about him. I struggled to believe in anything and I was uncertain about where home was for me.

I wanted to hire a psychiatrist to help me but I didn't. I needed to heal.

"What we run from has power over us."
— *Joyce Meyer*

I had to step out of a man's way I wasn't sure if he meant what he did drily or not. Whatever says the truth, the empire of pain tended to be built and I had to bounce back and keep my head above water surviving. The following months and years of the deepest spiritual work that I was compelled to do made me feel like jumping from my skin. I endured and thanks to the strong and hard background I came from, I managed to push it harder and start healing. I decided to forgive the incident and clear the mess that tried to haunt me because I wanted to move on and stand for the unbeatable self. I realized that I missed Nawres. I missed my parasympathetic and relaxed state. I wanted to be her again. And I knew that nobody was going to do me any favors or encourage me to save myself. It was my mission to dig myself out of that swamp.

Coaching myself to healing, was slow and killing.

I am not a therapist, but I am someone who has learned from her mistakes and these are the tools I have found to be effective for spiritual treatment.

Healing is possible and it happens one step at a time. It leads to personal expansion.

Forgive
As they say "To understand all is to forgive all."
Forgiveness is an immediate action. Do forgive yourself, the other part, and the incident. In doing so, you are cleaning your heart from poisonous emotions and preparing yourself for the healing trip. It is the former foundation. Without it, healing is impossible.

"Unforgiveness is like cancer. It will eat you from the inside out." I believe this saying of Jay Shetty says it all.

"And yet it's only the hidden that can terrify, not for what it's, but for its hiddenness."
 — A Course-Miracles

Vent Out Your Sadness

Speak your pain. Repressed pain triggers a deeper one. I suggest you never hold it inside. Don't do what I did. Vent out the unsaid and that can be through journaling, recording, or sharing it with someone you trust.

Here is the reason: shutting off feelings can get your health destroyed as it damages your immune system, consumes most if not all of your mental power, spoils the whole bloodstream with cortisol, and causes heart diseases.

"Remember a sore won't heal if it's covered. It needs fresh air to help the cells regenerate." In the words of Vex King.

Evaluate Your Emotions

You might think sitting with your feelings is not a great idea. However, it is the opposite. Assessing and evaluating your emotions will help you dismiss all the limiting and bad beliefs that trauma has brought you and made you see the world through. Dig deeper and remain searching within, so you clean all the dust and re-discover your dearest true self. It is your time-tested truth.

Take this seriously: you're not your feelings. And yes, evaluating your feelings is like licking your wounds. It won't be fun. We harbor pain and trauma if we don't study and speak to our emotions. They will keep on resurfacing. We fail later to start a new relationship. The heart remains closed, so why become the product of your past? Explore it all.

Be Humble

Don't feel bad for feeling bad. I understand you being tired and ill of the same sentiments. The important thing is never to go tough and rough on and with yourself, and expect trauma to visit you again and again. I advise you to open your hearts and believe in healing because it is possible.

"Chaos gives birth to dancing stars" is a saying of Friedrich Nietzsche that has served me well. Let it serve you too. Think about it being a positive trip. Perhaps you are going to love yourself more and become stronger than ever. Trust this, there is an equivalent forest of rewards after each hardship.

Choose the Relational Creatures

Surrounding yourself with reflective listeners, and dynamic and divine souls as a natural healing technique is the best. We become the people we surround ourselves with. Get for yourself a positive circle that can uplift your mood, protect your peace, save your motivation, and help you double your commitment. The one that can push you farther in life and believe in you. "The connectedness counters the pull of addictive behaviors" puts Bruce D. Perry in his way.

Shift the Focus

You've got the chance to rewrite your script. With trained and eager eyes, you can win over trauma. Sitting in your bed, unmoving, cutting off food, and indulging in alcohol whilst burning all of your mental power in whatever happened is not the way out.

It's a fact that being a trauma victim can get you closer to all forms of addiction.

The thing that helped me somewhat was writing. Every time I thought of him, I hit the pen and journal.

Grab a draft and write down certain activities or visions you want to achieve. Things you feel can help you regain some motivation. Get them crystal clear and start initiating small steps so you uplift yourself out of that depressing mood.

Sufficient Repetition

Instead of repeating the traumatic situation you faced and

helping it get integrated more into your subconscious, I suggest you bring in opposite beliefs and use them as a regular mantra:

"I am healing, I can get through this, I am strong enough, I can build a higher self."

Avoid the "I need to heal" as with that you're putting a lot of pressure on yourself. "Be it." Don't "want it."

Physical Therapy

The rhythm is an inspiring and effective therapeutic tool. So much of positive change can happen when you stimulate feel-good hormones in your brain so you repair those cells damaged by stress. Walking, dancing, working out, and moving in general do make the stress response system supple. You'll feel and function better. Guaranteed.

(More advanced healing techniques in my "Healing the Unhealed" master class.)

…Time passed and I started to feel reborn. I thought it was getting easier but I must share that I failed at having effective results from the first attempt. That is because I conducted the exercises above just once to find myself going through the same emotional war upon seeing (him) again. Honest, I had to start from scratch!

Metaphorically and scientifically speaking, seeing his face just inches away from mine and hearing his voice got my heart hammering like mad. I had a heavy rewind, a full-blown recollection of specific events. Flashbacks in which I felt like I was in a war. Everything triggered deep pain and tons of questions I couldn't overcome. It was all weird and intense. I don't know even if it was a trauma with big T or small t. I was so comfortable in my pain. Old wounds were triggered. It was all serving an evolutionary purpose.

Now after years, I realize that it's sometimes better to let someone go. That our past maybe wasn't the way it was. It's all in our minds and our hands. You might not believe this, but yes, the pain I had felt all those years was the result of my thinking. My thoughts had tortured me. This might seem surprising but there should be no self-blame because that's just a silly game your mind wants you to play. Any story can be seen this way or the other way, and in the end, it's all about your perception.

The perception that is already in your subconscious.

My post-traumatic wisdom can't be rawer than this: Healing isn't something you do in your spare time. You have to maintain good observation and effort at all times. There must be a serious commitment. And it is your job to heal yourself.

Perhaps your parents spoke to you in a way that caused you to feel very bad, you lost a loved one, you had a devastating accident that has made you disabled or you got physically abused in your childhood.

From a position of understanding, the traumatic situations are different and unique for each person but common in sequence: a severe internal soreness.

Even the experiences that we choose to describe as bad can ultimately help us for good as they clarify our thinking. (I'm finding a way out of my relationship now).

Get up and stand for yourselves because you are braver than what you think! You're more than what you think you can be.

You must not become affected. You must not become a slave. You must resist and rebel as you let go of what's not serving you anymore.

You must survive and move on for that stupendous race.

To Make Your LEAP
To Jump from Drudge to Super

I appreciate the past for:

The better degree of consciousness.
The stupendous redirection.
Becoming stronger.
The regal upshots.
The thumping transformation
Helping me regain trust in being.
Turning me into a better archer.
Supercharging me.
Resetting the inner confidence on fire.

I hate the past for:

The murdering sense of guilt.
Being left behind.
The slaughtering pain.
The double-minded thoughts.
The smashed belief.
The unfaithful people I encountered.
The time wasted.
The unbearable discord.

Hatred or appreciation. To be healed or tormented. You choose.

Chapter 8

Give Me Liberty or Give Me Death

"I wasn't most people. I had a different take on the real world."
– Nims Purja

"You're not going to the gym at this time. It's late," my brother said while glaring at me.

"I am going. And for your information, Mom knows," I said in response whilst trying to control my temper.

"I said you're not going anywhere. It's evening. The car won't go out," he shouted.

I couldn't do what Thomas Erikson advises us to do: "You help people understand you by creating an awareness." There I found this, "I can give you knowledge, but I can't make you think."

A look of rebellion and "How dare you yell at me" washed over my face, daring him even to continue arguing. I narrowed my eyes in his direction to say "Mind your own business." If Mom hadn't interrupted then, maybe blood would have arrived on the scene. That confrontation was more efficient than I expected. It lit a fuse in me. The fire deep inside me melted away every bit of self-esteem and respect. Remaining consistent with my routine then meant a lot to me. Skipping it for senseless reasons would starve my ego and jeopardize my focus and my nature would never tolerate such behavior.

I have always had my parents' backing but never my brother's support. Since secondary school graduation, my relationship that joins me with him has taken a different road. Before, it was jam-packed with troubles and Dos and Don'ts. Telling me not to do what I wanted to do: "Behave," "The dress is too short," and "Watch yourself."

He had a bit of rebellion in him just as I did. He always saw me through the lens of flaws. And of course, I wouldn't listen or comply.

Psychologically speaking, that's called "reactance," an unpleasant feeling that emerges when people experience a threat to or loss of their free behavior.

My reactance was more of the "independent reactance" which reflects our deeper desire to make our own choices. It can't be easily influenced by the social network.

While the "defiant reactance" is more about impulsively doing the opposite of what we're told to do.

Shifting my focus was hard as not to think of that negative environment. Simple questions like "How can I do/change this" are way better than "I am hating this."

That question reminded me over and over again of what I believed in.

Being uninterested in the traditional routes to life, I couldn't pretend to be enjoying what others set for me. I couldn't accept it being rosy. I had a whole completely different world in my mind that had taken him so long to understand and digest. On some days, I felt I would prefer to be dead than to show up for a conversation with him. I scolded myself for thinking such risk-taking thoughts. There, my mind could lead me from anything to just run. On my high school completion day, the first question he asked me was, "Did you fail?" followed by, "As if you've won the World Cup."

"No," I said, baffled by the disappointment to still hear more. It hit me somewhere and I vividly can still remember. The feeling of unworthiness was buried deep. I felt the ground moving beneath me. I wished he could see what a huge and interesting step it was for me. I didn't expect such a response on that day specifically out of all days. Truly, you need to be a bit more emotionless to feel no pain or be drifted by such setbacks. I wished he pretended even for a second to support one of my decisions, talks, and visions. We have never spoken about those days, but I know he holds a lot of guilt for that. The "cognitive' and "emotional empathy" were missing. That ability to understand the beliefs, habits, thoughts, and emotions, the other person is having. This didn't take place. On the other side, there comes a time when you look in the mirror and realize that you don't have to be the one who's always trying to make others cope with you. You've got to save yourself.

That was a fact and not a belief.

The village and the school I grew up in were neither the less. Lame instructions, silly superstitions, boloney gossip, and gender discrimination were all present. That clouds the heart and mind. It was for me the environment of repressed talents and gifts. In my own book of life, at least.

I grew up hearing the word "luck" very often. There were times when I really started thinking that I was not lucky. Those doing good in life had things I didn't have. That I was stuck in life and nothing right was going on. That my destiny was non-changeable and my choices were limited. And I hated that I wasn't born with a silver spoon in my mouth. Then I didn't realize that it was one of society's myths. A delusion we have been programmed to use and live by. An excuse we use when life doesn't go the way we want. A mask we wear to hide rejection and failure. I didn't know that "luck" is about being able to find out what you love and work wholeheartedly for it. I was blind to see that it's all about making choices and grabbing possibilities that are wise and alternative enough. That we have to be perfectly ready and agile to analyze the signs and I didn't know that a silver spoon is not gifted but it's in my power to create. The same thing led me to this deep observation today: Is Elon Musk lucky to be a billionaire? Is Chris Anderson lucky to be TED's president and head curator? Is Priyanka Chopra lucky to become a global artist? Is Rehan Yar Khan lucky to build the Flora 2000 company? Those luminaries challenged the norms and dug out their paths. They have been curious and serious about their fields. They have kept on learning and knocking on doors. They have remained loyal to their exceptionality. They have persisted on the tough roads and set epic strategies. To be brutally honest, this seems obvious to me, but at that time, it was an imminent big problem. "Luck" or "magic" is truly a belief that can drain all of your resources leaving you with nothing to bounce back on. This is because the risk of misunderstanding is very high with no resources left to recover. Indeed, it stands in stark contrast to what society encourages us to do.

Another icing on the cake was the myth of age. So many of those days didn't make me feel that I could do something apart from going to school and taking exams. I don't know but from an early age, I've been an observer. I refuse to close my heart and silence my intuition.

I choose not to be prodded by the shepherd. I won't allow myself to become affected and poleaxed by what I am told. Instead, I would always do what my intuition asks me to do. I would be very picky with whom I surround myself and talk freely with. I have been teaching myself to think that way and the same attitude has eventually been powering me onto the next summit I strive to reach. Shaking it all away is my everyday mission and that is my force shield. I am not bad-mouthing anybody under any circumstances because I respect this very important fact: We are relational creatures and our earliest and current developmental experiences are based on our connections.

"Magic is just someone spending more time on something that anyone else might reasonably expect."
– Raymond Joseph Teller

That means, emotionally, mentally, and physically, we need mingling.

But I am also a firm believer in this:

To understand magic, one must have the right people to see magic as "when you stop seeing the crowd, you become a part of it," greatly said by Ron Malhotra.

Find the community that doesn't question you. That doesn't question your abilities and happiness.

A real fighter has to be enfolded and enwrapped with supportive spirits to get him regaining the trust he might have lost in the brighter and nobler future. Euphoric and colorful which can help with seeing opportunities and spotlighting optimism everywhere. Supportive to respect his intriguing visions and see him winning and orchestrating a life of marvel... Like-minded and clever to discuss and share with him ideas and not rumors. Sensible enough to mentor him in great ways and push him to snatch chances as a supreme opportunist. Applaud him for even the smallest things he does... Seeing within him unlimited potential because "all it takes is someone to believe in you" [in the words of Oprah Winfrey]. Elevating and uplifting him to see outside his front door and thus drawing him outside his limitations. People may call you "crazy" for taking risks and abandoning the norms. How many times did you stop yourself from doing something just because someone told you that you can't? That your genetics are challenged. That you're not the next Einstein or Friedrich Nietzsche? Didn't you feel belittled and negative? Didn't you adopt the same until it became a part of your belief system? I had to fight for the fairy tales and stop myself from wearing those lenses everybody wore. What's essential and super important to mention is that their impossibilities become your limits.

We often imbibe such myths into our mindset. until they become our reality and destiny. And this is one of the biggest issues because you are smarter than you think. Seeing so many having the tools and methods but not the right thinking patterns is a big struggle. If you are here with me, I want to tell you that you can unleash so much of what you have. You can break records too and do what wasn't been done before. There is a lot within you and you've got to show it. You've got to stop believing the false assumptions. You've got to unlearn them and say stop to the "age," "genius," and "functional" illusions. You've got to say yes to "The Myth Breaker" mindset. You've got to believe in you. Fathoming this: It's not their fault. They've been brainwashed, taught to adopt but not to think. Honest. The word "society" gets thrown around a lot. But there is so much unexpressed and unexpected out there. So many sets and circles. So many patriarchal norms, outdated traditions, unnecessary worrying fences, and doubting voices. The aura smells of demotivation and mediocrity as parodies seem to be ubiquitous. For much of our childhood and adult days, we have adopted things we're not. We've given up on gazillions of dreams. And here's this: we've been diverted to run the wrong races. It's so easy to follow the rules than to question them. It's easy to eat from the tray you've been served and believe it is the way it is. Taking this into account, "We are what we see. We are the products of our surroundings."

We become our friends and environs and such force is transmissible as we adopt each other's feelings and ideas. Much of our family, society, culture, and genes are playing a big part in that.

Transgenerational Transmission is the exact right term to use here. Someone's fear can become yours. For example, if you were born into a family that fears change and has a bad perception of it, you'll eventually adopt the same even when you have no real present experiences. A major part of our brain is continually monitoring other people around us. Being involved in the course of understanding how those around us think and feel, we're in a way consciously and unconsciously absorbing so much of emotions and insights. Thoughts of a stressed person's state become yours if you stay with him for too long. Now think of your workplace, of someone energetic and vivid. Wouldn't you spend your day with this person of peerless motivation as if you've taken a dose of endorphins? When we hang out with this person for a decent amount of time, we start using the same words he's using and habits he's adopting. Your ingrained bases are being challenged. And that's just the beginning because with repetition such encounters become tremendous determinants.

The dilemma somewhat resides with your boss, partner, or parents. Those whom you see and deal with every day. Despite all the inner work you've done and the awareness you have incorporated, you will still be influenced and affected. We're like sponges, sucking languages, ideas, beliefs, and habits (both good and bad) from the pictures in magazines we see, books we read, and people we meet and get along with. We see, feel, learn, and then pass on what we have navigated.

The society into which you were born and perhaps which still cradles you in its arms is obviously affecting how you function for the rest of your life. It's affecting how you run your own race. Making it here today, finally understanding that it's not only about who you are, but whom you know as well. In running your race, you need to decide whom to follow and whom to unfollow. What to take and what to offload. You need to decide either to belong or not to belong. To live freely or die in chains.

Put your oxygen mask on first before helping others.

Dare to Offload

To save yourself from this:
- Living with inner stress
- Doubting and giving up on ideas and abilities
- Feeling enfeebled and demotivated
- Losing sight and hope in life
- Becoming double-minded
- Believing in issues and complications
- Spotlighting negativity and impossibilities everywhere

You've got to do this:
- Lessen the face-to-face contact as the vibe is higher when it's live
- Listen when it's obliged, yet adopt it if it suits your goals
- Remain distant and maintain your personal space
- Don't argue much. Save the mental power
- Write to release the adopted bad feelings (as soon as you feel them)
- Spend time doing uplifting activities

Race barefoot and dare to offload what might weigh you down.

Chapter 9

Silencing any Talk of the Worst

"Do not speak badly of yourself for the warrior within hears your words and is lessened by them."
— Old Japanese Samurai Proverb

It might be surprising to reveal that pessimism is also internal.

By going on the journey, maybe you're too sharp and hard on yourself for not having a good grade, failing at getting your dream job, being an unsuccessful partner, and gaining weight. You might be going foolishly to stand in front of the mirror and assume only seeing the outraged reflection of you shouting, and pointing a finger back at you:

"You're stupid, you're not good enough, you're not valued, you're a loser, you can't overcome this…"

I've been there. I feel you.

Having said that, you're getting yourself mentally blocked.

I personally grew up in an environment where those mandatory positive inner talks were not valued. We had never thought that what's impressed inside of us could be expressed.

All future strides were addressed with "What if someone kidnaps you?" "What if you fail?"

"What if it doesn't work?"

"What if you get robbed?" "What if he's lying?"

"What if you're not meant for that?"

Those are the same mantras I had been fed for long. I would hear it almost every day like a lullaby.

I must admit that sometimes parents love you but at the same time they don't know how to love you.

The talks can be found in the most educated families. In my book, I call them the talks of "what if+ negative outcome."

"Your face is looking pale. Are you falling sick? See I told you. That's because you didn't listen to me last night. It was super cold, and you insisted on removing your jacket. You ignored me. What will happen to your exams tomorrow if you wake up with a fever?" Mom shouted at me once.

She called my sister and told her about the prediction. "Mom, I'm okay. I feel nothing. And please wish me well.

Why do you have to predict the worst always?"

"Can't you see your face in the mirror?" She said as she rushed me to the toilet so I could have a look at my face.

I could see nothing but my messy hair bun. I had neither signs nor symptoms. But I started to freak out. A rush of anxiety came over me.

It was an odd expectation sinking in and provoking within me a sense of fear, and I went with it. It triggered the stress response system. My 'amygdala' started alerting me.

"What am I supposed to do now? There's no way out," I mumbled whilst talking to myself.

I started feeling what my mother told me. I pictured and lived it in my imagination with all senses integrated. I felt it until I saw it. The affirmative method was with focused attention.

I literally started preparing myself for staying home the next day and not going to school.

The words were echoed moment after moment, hour after hour.

The gale of fear was monumental. It ravaged and hampered

my hope for the best.

My state eventually changed rapidly for the worse after that morning. I must confess, that my inner speech did hold me back from being healthy and giving my exams.

I should have conjectured a better outcome.

And so, what happened was because I listened and adopted what was told to me and not because she had the foresight.

That's because I overthought it and conveyed the "hetero suggestion" to an "auto-suggestion." Masking the fear of "what's next" with "let's hope for the best" won't help you. Trust me.

Digging deeper, there's something called the subconscious or irrational mind; a super-intelligent part of the brain that has a huge impact on our actions. It doesn't argue. It is just there to implement our thoughtful commands. Try thinking about something a million times over and see if you don't get it sooner or later. It's that magical. Another interesting thing about the unconscious mind is that it doesn't sleep. It remains up the whole night to function your heartbeat, blood circulation, and digestion. To help you receive wisdom and solutions whilst connecting with your conscious mind: your tool to communicate with the outside world.

When the mind gets impressed by an optimistic idea, the race takes the vibe. It takes the overdrive.

…And "it's an astonishing and subtle truth that the law of the subconscious mind works for good and bad ideas alike."

Saying that, your thoughts can make you happy, but they can also make you sad, emphasized Joseph Murphy.

Lots of people aren't getting better and that goes to this ubiquitous fact: The mind is constantly bombarded with the material world. The world of "hustle and bustle." News from here, family and friends' point of view from there. Toxic fuel is available everywhere.

What people also don't know and what I also grew up being ignorant about is what we call the mind-body connection. We don't know that our thoughts also affect our physical state.

And for another realization: Your thoughts affect your feelings. Your feelings affect what happens inside your body. In return, you start to make choices as your body language and behavior gets affected.

There's a divine power hiding behind the mind and leading the body.
How many sicknesses were the seeds of negative thoughts? And how many illnesses were cured mentally and left science wondering. **Your inner talk can be the stepping stone.**

I didn't know about this mindset culture until the age of twenty when I read a book I grabbed randomly from one of the bookstores, *The Power of Your Subconscious Mind* written by Joseph Murphy. It talks about self-talk and its operation in healing, creating marvels and opportunities such as success and wealth. It brings to the table mental blocks and human relations.
The one masterpiece that's worth reading over and over again.
Major realizations began to set in. Before that, my gut was always taking the lead. It was reliable enough I can say but discovering the power of my subconscious mind is something else. It's different. They both work hand in hand.
Knowing that made me realize that nothing is impossible. That the future can be malleable. That we are our life authors.
I profusely speak energy. Whoever knows me, knows this very well. I find my subconscious ready to do anything to give

up on what I grew up hearing repeatedly. Ready to clean my energy and back me up with: "How would they know? Remain bullish."

Everything happening around me is being led by my mind and the code I'm reading to myself. What I'm materializing today is not coincidental. It was once but a simple thought backed with lots of love, belief, and confidence.

I respectfully honor my irrationality for all the hard work.

Today, I can't tell you that I don't think harmfully at times or that I don't get chaotic thoughts, but I'm happy to always be back to the right way, the "back-to-track" way. I feel jubilant to have the keys to constantly turn and search inward.

Acumen is not to recognize all the ways, but to choose your words and ideas carefully. Yeah, we can't contemplate a world without some toxic news and influences. We can understand how self-talk impacts how we see ourselves and hence life.

Can you imagine your outcomes if you are feeling impossibilities and sluggishness?

I can imagine. The times in my life when I visualized hellish scenarios and they tended to happen and how they were the ugliest and creepiest.

Unexamined, I tortured myself a lot with useless ideas.

I notice every time I criticize money, I end up losing it. Or every time I start my day with dreary and erratic energy, my day unfolds in an unbalanced and unhappy manner.

If for any reason, someone tells you that the worst days are ahead, remember that you are a magnet for what you desire in life. So, give a voice to all that is encouraging and elevating.

If I ask you now not to think of your desk for example, will you not immediately think of it?

That's what happens often when we go saying, "I don't

want to lose my money," "I don't want to get hurt... I don't want to become fat."

The results are going to be the opposite. Your brain admires pictures. It will keep hunting around to find the memory that can recreate that "I don't want" command you're giving it. To put it differently, your brain automatically deletes "I don't" so you're left with "I want."

A negative sentence can only give you negative results.

True that your brain doesn't like negative thoughts. I believe you can imagine what can happen as you choose the negative language that is creating negative images for you. **The quality of your inner language determines the quality of your life.**

It works as your reality machine maker.

Your subconscious takes you through three stages as you receive the information from the external world:

1- Delete: Your mind deletes all information that does not match your needs.

2- Distort: Your mind distorts some of the information based on your values and beliefs.

3- Generalize: Your mind categorizes the information according to what it is already familiar with.

That's how your view of the world is created. Your inner talk plays a big role in this internal process.

Trust me: if you believe you can do something, you will do it. Your subconscious will create a way for you. It will **delete** anything that might not serve you.

Since ninety-five percent of what we do is subconscious (as per Bruce Lipton's research), your deepest thoughts are dominating. It's all about how you talk to yourself. The inner conversation says a lot about the baggage you're holding.

It's defining your relationship with everything around you. It says a lot about you.

What also happens on the way is that we are too attached to what we have been, to the same software that may be running out of date now. If you get excited about any idea, ensure that you know any better, so you take it seriously.

Have a look around and observe someone who's brilliant at some task, and then study the facts. You'll find that the decision and vision of becoming have already been made subconsciously.

And thus, you choose. Either to be motivated by your uplifting codes or to be demotivated by your negative thoughts. Maybe it's time to change the codes now.

Distract yourself as soon as a negative idea pops up. Get up and dance. Clap your hands or maybe just jump out of your idea. Importantly, block the way to the law of your mind. That's the law of repetition.

"The harmony between thought and reality can be found in the grammar of the language."
— Wittgenstein

With your inner language, you write your narrative. I'm not against any God-like power, but remember that you're a piece of your deity. Therefore, you can make up your own story.

With the aid of positive thinking, you can materialize wonders. Track your way of thinking and silence any talk of the worst.

The Preventive Steps:

Increase Your Self-Awareness:
Most problems arise when people lack self-awareness. Think about someone shouting and being aggressive during an interesting job meeting for just feeling bored, or someone hitting a car on the road while being engaged on a phone call.

The same things apply to the negative affirmations that one addresses himself with. If the person is mindful and thoughtful, he can never commit such a crime.

Awareness, dear racers is everything!

It is then important to hear your mind and monitor your feelings. There you should spot your expressions, remain calm for a while, and research their nature and origin: your irrational mind is full of memories related to previous emotions and old experiences. And so, your reaction towards certain situations partially, if not completely, is based on the previous projections.

Clean Up Your Subconscious Mind:
Once you become conscious of the concept of your irrational mind and the impact of the affirmations you are choosing, you can clean it from any bad past events or limiting and discouraging beliefs. You can start seeing the situation through realistic and valid eyes.

The result: the mind is able to blossom with better, greater, and nobler ideas!

Implement Positive Auto Suggestions:
From a position of understanding the auto-suggestions being the mechanism of your subconscious mind, I believe you can propose positive and uplifting ones.

I confess that negative affirmations are inevitable. It is very tough to get rid of them completely.

But you have the tool too! You know very well how to silence any talk of the worst now.

The best advantage of this method is that you implement it before sleep. It is the best time for your mind to get recharged and bring about the best guidance.

Your Possibility Pillars
- I am a possibilitarian
- I am smart
- I am learning
- Good things are about to happen to me
- I am poised
- I have a bright future ahead
- I am consistent and unrelenting
- I am goal-oriented
- I am a believer
- I am confident
- All I need is coming my way
- I'm guided

Remember life is fair. You get what you focus on and discuss ***the whole time… So express confidence, intelligence, and optimism.***

What if +~~negative outcome~~ positive outcome

Chapter 10

Different Sets in Play

"You can't make an omelet without breaking eggs."
– English Proverb

"Do you think you have the right balance? Or is it too heavy on one side?" goes Abel Antony in his book *The Tears of An Indian Cabin Crew*."

This question captures the life-changing importance of understanding ourselves profoundly at every turn.

"Yourself" or "Myself" are not as simple as they might seem to be. They're deep. They're a whole complete world.

And that means, whatever the circumstance, your race won't go any better because it takes the whole lead from you. It leaps from within.

For so long, I had been too single-minded, thinking life was just about mentally growing and financially expanding. I had thought a strong mindset was the only important thing.

Being smart, successful, and unstoppable would only require potent ideas and creations.

I even found it utterly hard to acknowledge anything else apart from what I believed in; Mastery is earned.

That's what happens when you have been attached to how you have been for too long. When you ignore that there's indeed another part of you that's not growing. That's fixed.

Until I found out that it has but a small role in the life I am crafting because I am not just a mind. I am more than that.

My entire life span has started reeking of new changes and enhancements on discovering Robin Sharma's method "The Four Interior Empires." Adopting it has helped me get better control over my race.

"Together, these four private arenas form the foundation of the true primal power that rests inside every human being alive today. Most of us have disowned and discredited this formidable force as we've spent our days pursuing things outside our worlds," he states.

When I read this for the first time, I witnessed a hint of realization in the sky which I took as a wakeup call. My brain flashed a million thoughts. My neural circuit was on fire.

I spent the rest of my day thinking and understanding that to become the best I can be, four complete elements must be regained and polished. That must be managed.

Later that evening, I set off a new plan. A new area of interest and upturns. "My life will soon improve," I affirmed.

This can explain why so many people work hard but don't get lucky in life and why lots of people out there are empty voids and pursuing harmful connections. It's by far the reason why the race can be a bit harder, and so impossible to run for them.

No one taught us how to look interiorly and why it is so vital to do that.

Melt an iceberg and you'll see what inhabits you.

What you're indeed made of. What truly matters.

After an intense workout this morning that I thought to skip but I didn't, I recalled the time when I was stingy with my health.

Two years back, I had severe hair loss. The problem might sound common for those living in the UAE because of the desalinated water and vitamin D insufficiency. That wasn't my case and anyhow that's a myth we're still unsure of.

It was falling all over in my hands, on the floor, in the bathroom, and everywhere. In the beginning, I assumed I was having a common hair loss triggered by changing the shampoo or using an ironing machine frequently.

It felt like a never-ending war cleaning my room almost every day.

What was even worse was those empty bald spots in the front of my head. I could see my scalp appearing larger every next day. I was terrified that I would wake up one day and find it all on my pillow.

The same was observed by my friends and colleagues. Their concerns stopped me in my tracks.

So, it was a two-way thing: either become entirely bald or go to the doctor and get an examination done.

"Have you had a recent shock or are you stressed about something?" the doctor asked.

"No, thank God... I can't complain about my life," I said. "If that's not the case, then do you exercise and eat healthy?" He carried on with his investigation. "Yes," I replied confidently.

"I can provide you with some shampoos and hair sprays but first we have to do a full-body check-up for further analysis. We need to know the status of your blood cells and hormones," he suggested.

After one week, the results came out. I had inadequate Vitamin D which is the case with eighty percent if not a hundred percent of all UAE residents due to the climate.

Everything else from B12 to red and white blood cells was totally fine.

For that, he gave me a prescription for some injections, hair rinses, and sprays as a treatment.

The cure given didn't make me confident about the real reason. Something was missing. That day I knew that I had lied not only to the doctor but to myself too when he asked if I was stressed out about something.

Deep down, I knew that I was lying. I could feel that there was something wrong happening in my life. Something I was repressing and keeping very close to my heart. I was off balance.

When I wrote my first book, it was too hot on the feet of my breakup. I was also seeking approvals and pushing harder for my growth at the workplace, but things were very slow and tough.

I was putting in the hours every day and fighting for my finances and ideas. I was walking with my vision fixed on my future. Nonstop.

My mind was always busy and so focused that I didn't allow it to think about my health. I wasn't giving myself the proper care my body deserved.

I work hard for everything I want and I am still doing that to this day. Obviously.

It's in my nature that I like to double and triple-check my work for every small detail (I am doing this even when I am writing this book for you).

I take my life seriously because I believe in this: "If you don't take yourself seriously, no one will. Seriously." [as said by Robin Sharma]

That was a lot for my brain to adjust to. I was placing lots of pressure on myself and didn't realize that I was killing it softly.

I have to confess: I was very generous with my mindset and completely stingy with my health.

Learning a big lesson, I decided it would be the last day I would be stingy with myself.

I made up my mind to push as hard for my health as I did for my vision. I have ever since been giving my body the rest it requires to be ahead of the stress game.

Without health, there is no point. No point coming in. No point making anything. Without it, we are all whistling in the dark.

Your health is your tool for getting the job done – whatever it happens to be. Without it, we are an empty page waiting to be written.

By that intake, I have progressed and started with my "soulset." I took my first steps towards it when the people who got laid off during the pandemic, the poor ones back home, the family, the strangers, the pets in the street, and even the watchman of my building started concerning me a lot.

The general despair started making me think; Was I too selfish? Was I living in a bubble?

I was already in a way ready to start over.

You can't just go to work, reap the money, and horde to end up with a big bank balance. Well, you can do that but probably you won't get it right. Two things will matter when you are on your deathbed: Did you realize the reason you were born for? And how many people have you helped?

Floating in the dizzying material stream of life and its crosscurrents, humans have become too selfish to help, trapped in that routine of earning and saving as if our conscious is mortgaged to money.

I thought back to the most memorable advice my father gave me. It was during my early days at primary school "Many people say don't give money, give food instead. But I don't agree with this because giving is what comes from the heart and that's important."

I felt very bad and unsatisfied. I had missed a big amount of inner peace for quite a long time.

Taking a harder line with myself was devilishly difficult, and it took me time to be aware of the mess my ego had created. An ego that was being fed through the pain, past traumatic encounters, and insecure feelings of guilt, doubt, and fear.

I may not have valued the word "Ego" that much during high school when I first knew about Freud, the philosopher.

Looking back, I see that those early classroom lessons have returned to teach me again. I decided to stick out and push harder to remain a student, humble, and calm.

Relatively later, when my "heartset" balance got jeopardized and pitched me on collapsing, I fought like a beast for that new environment and those norms.

I predicted those new sets in play to be exactly triggering out trips of deep evaluation and so often more uneasiness. Gladly, I passed through them all. In so many ways, it took a lot of courage.

But why? These were some of the most important places that I had less interest in and obviously, the new philosophy presented an opportunity for me to work through it all.

A beacon of light to spotlight things I had neglected and cared less about.

Having it a little easier, each step caused me to pause and overthink every now and ever.

I wanted more balance. That's when I noticed the new changes, the new sets in play, and a different part of life.

Here's the thing, the race cannot be owned if there is no

inner concord or accord. It cannot be captured if the heart is still suffering and ruthless. It cannot be ruled if the health is poor. It cannot be managed if the ego is dominating. It cannot be controlled if the potentials are shackled, and the fun is not being taken.

Life has a very fair accounting system and "what we let is what will continue."

Chapter 11

Honor Your Hecklers

"Until pains are endured, depressions surmounted, mockeries ignored, and goliaths conquered, destiny might not be achieved."
— Ikechukwu Izuakor

"She's a villager," "Your standards are too high," "Use simple words," "You're living in the La La Land," and "She has some attitude."

So much was said to me as a joke whilst I know it wasn't.

Yeah, me and the hecklers have come a long way.

So, like many, my parents gave me everything. They supported me in all possible ways.

My childhood was balanced, rosy, and bountifully spent. I grew up wearing good clothes and being served with my favorite food on the table. I couldn't ask for more.

However, today, I have some regret for blaming them one day for not having the privilege of owning a big family name or the resources to buy a house in the city.

My early primary and secondary school days got me bullied.

My ability to be congruent and brave to reveal it all today is my true strength.

I was the girl who people always laughed at for her audacity.

The girl who people always disrespected for being a village dweller.

We grew up in a small northern township and everybody knew that. We kept much to ourselves and were thankful. We believed in self-respect and had an incredible father who committed his life a million times over but for us. Due to him, we were able to study and live in the best conditions.

Then, respect was measured by the answer to this question "Where do you live?". We were pigeonholed and treated as per that.

According to society, being "dusky" wasn't to the liking of most people. Hashtag racism.

Every day was a bullying day. For no reason, I would hear insensitive mockeries from the bus station itself. I would count every minute to reach home so I could feel protected and safe.

Navigating that for almost a decade, I don't think any person anywhere could handle it.

Words that kept playing in my mind for long which I started to believe in were: "I'm dusky, I'm fat. I'm a villager. I'm not special. I'm just a piece of shit."

I had those feelings of insecurity and unworthiness which were buried deep down. There was a certain pang of remorse for things I didn't commit.

I was afraid if I even coughed, I would be criticized for that. I even had to think twice before liking someone.

Whatever I lacked, started to affect me. I almost cut a piece of myself. Crazy how parodies aren't your fault, but you take their responsibility.

I doubled the confidence and resilience to wake up daily and show up for school.

My family wasn't that much concerned with whatever I was facing. Between paying the electricity bills, clearing debts, and securing a good financial living for us, there was little time to focus on what was happening to me mentally.

Respect was something I earned myself. I was every teacher's favorite student for the good part of my school years.

My confidence was another flotation device to help me keep my head above and breathe. It was my everyday accessory. Perhaps, I would feel sad and get offended, but I would never give up on my potent personality. I would keep my mouth pretty shut, but I would never walk in fear. I would be seen as "unstoppable."

But deep down, I was craving for acceptance. I then turned to make external changes. I trimmed my eyebrows and changed my hair color after uncountable fights with my mother. I lost count of the days I stole my sister's makeup kit and applied all that was available to lighten my skin color. I can now see the humor in this situation: I would run from the sun and lock myself home for days trying to make my skin lighter.

I became someone I wasn't.

With that already made, I thought I would fit in. Yet, the criticism never stopped.

Right before the class, someone would say: "Try your best to lose weight. You're too rounded. Please tie back your hair, it's not suiting you."

"This eyeliner of yours is so ugly. Remove it." Another added, "Her English isn't that good."

It was the environment of rude boys and bad girls.

This continued even in my teenage years. They couldn't affect me more, but so many comments and mockeries are still being brought to me.

Until a realization that came to me in the last few years after working through negativity.

Since the age of seventeen, I've returned to my normal life and self. I've returned to my skin. I've stopped caring and accepted myself for simply being myself.

Having done that, I've felt blessed to save so many special traits. And today, I'm sure enough.

"What happened to you can be your power."
- Oprah Winfrey

Suddenly, the world stopped being a devil because my perception of it changed.

I railed against the unfairness of it all. For a little while, it was shocking to me that I had considered giving up on so much. I realized that I didn't have to fit in. I wondered what was hurting me.

Now, it doesn't feel too painful looking back at those days. I confess. Embracing my authentic version then is helping me today. It turned out to be a great move. I actually would love to honor every attacker I've met on the way. Maybe I would never accept and respect myself this much without you.

I am proud of the choice I made to be the woman I am today, guiding me every step of the way.

And I don't consider it to be traumatic. I neither hold grudges. I've learned to distance myself without hurting myself.

Spreading the message, take this chance to look closely at yourself and digest this simple truth: You are a special "touch" nobody can touch.

People will mock you for justified and mostly unjustified reasons. So why bother?

And if you're not powered enough by self-love then you will be easy prey to the hecklers. As humans, we will sometimes doubt ourselves. We will face criticism and wonder if it's worth it to keep on trying.

You might be thinking; It feels heavy. Should I just skip or accept it?

Accept through skipping it. You don't have to run from this very important fact:

The early days and experiences are molding and shaping the way we are living today and will live tomorrow. There are lots of unseen, exiled feelings and memories. You've got to be aware of what you're running from.

You deserve to be seen, cared for, and healed. In the end, nobody can run forever.

And in the meantime, you don't have to worry much about it.

I will never know what people used to feel pleasure with.

But I will forever know this for sure; we don't have to fit in. We don't have to be understood. And it's okay to be mistaken for weirdness, over-confidence and insanity. It's okay to be different. It's okay to be happy in your skin that you were brought into this world with.

The inner gratification should and must be put first without negotiation. That's the number one rule because if you have peerless self-respect and faith, there's absolutely nothing that can demoralize you.

Forever, we can't please them all.

And if someone tends to do that, understand he is giving up on his standards and principles for the sake of being a people pleaser.

The truly amazing truth is this: to be ridiculed and laughed at is the price a racer gets the moment he creates a unique sphere for himself. It's the moment he decides to be different and chooses the best for himself and not them. It's the same moment he listens to his truths and chooses that prominent path.

Let them laugh. Let them gossip. Let them know that it's far more than impossible to control a potent racer.

Shut the ears, fill the heart with a deep belief, and get moving because they will write you off as a loudmouth in one way or another, and the doubting voices will fill the room regularly.

In a world that has brainwashed us to behave as the rest when we should not, remain true to the sterling values and know that Benjamin Franklin was right when he said, "To be yourself in a world that is constantly trying to make you something else is the **greatest accomplishment.**"

So, be yourself, everyone else is taken.

Chapter 12

Confidence Is Your Horse

"The only thing you need to wear well is your confidence."
     – Priyanka Chopra

"You're confident and charismatic." The one sentence I hear whenever I talk to people and walk into rooms.

It's the same sentence that I've been often praised for.

My four-year-old self could navigate and feel that. It was an early childhood experience that could honor the part. Yeah. During my kindergarten days, the idea of packing my bag and running out from home came to my mind and moved through me. I don't know how I managed to place an undergarment and bottle of water in my small backpack and from where I learned that poised walk and gathered the audacity to open the door and say to my family: "I'm going far, far away."

It's like I have always wanted to make my way.

If my parents hadn't stopped and caught me then, only my Deity knows what could have happened.

I know it sounds silly and funny, but I believe it was a confidence-boosting and bullet-proofing stride.

When you learn confidence, you no longer have to run from anything or anyone.

I made a lot of choices that set me free. I spoke to my unspeakable fears. I crossed miles alone, went for long night drives alone, climbed and jumped from heights alone, met strangers alone, ate at restaurants alone, and cried messy tears alone.

Confidence is something you learn and model alone, and then you go out to the world and celebrate it.

Unfortunately, it's not something everybody chooses. They have this idea that confidence does toughen and unsoften your edges. Like it's a way to numb out the constant pressure, unrevealed trauma, or addictions.

They don't see it as a necessary route everyone has to be willing to take so they can begin to free themselves too.

It doesn't come to their minds that for instance "the longer we hold on to fears, the more they ferment until eventually they become toxic," as Jay Shetty said.

That fear in all its forms, whether short or long termed, whether it's caused by attachment or failure will always leave us retreating and half paralyzed.

It is blocking and disconnecting us from our abilities at a time when we have a lot to offer to our races.

It's akin to a fire. Once ignited, it will eat you from the inside out.

"Ahh. Now you're starting to be delinquent." "Shush. You can't talk."

"Is this how she walks?" "Who's she?"

"She's bossy."

"I suggest you better go down to their level."

Why do we have to make a call to work against confidence? and not fear?

Why do we have to mistake confidence for negative superiority?

Why do we have to label someone's confidence with shame and unhealthy perfectionism?

Some people call it "overconfidence." I call it a strong belief system.

Recognizing the worthiness of doing it, I can say that's constantly about how you want to feel. And importantly it's not something you were born with, it's something you grow and build over time. Some might be more self-assured than others, and again that has nothing to do with supernatural powers as confidence is not gifted. It's gained and practiced.

It's about taking the opportunities you see in front of you and unshackling your best efforts.

When you do that, you can serve, inspire, and help others.

So where does confidence come from?

In my life book, it comes from the knowledge of you knowing what you are capable of.

As we discovered earlier: What you think of yourself is what you should be concerned about.

If you want to feel confident, how often do you think that you can make it?

Have a deeper look at the way you're talking to yourself.

I have been confident for as long as I can remember.

It comes from knowing your strengths and areas of improvement. It often comes from competency as well: your skills and experiences.

The sad part is this: The lack of self-confidence is what creates barriers and limits.

Confidence expands your impact. It's a vision you must embrace.

Why not write your code: your code of confidence? We all love superheroes for their confidence, I believe. So why not become the next superhero?

Confidence is in the head. It's a song that you can play. Let's try it out and see how it goes. If you play it whenever and wherever you go, you will do great things.

But most importantly, it gives you great compassion. A compassion that can carry you further while experiencing the fears of the world.

No matter how much you've struggled or suffered, kicking it off is your superpower. It's your horse to travel fast and far. It's the glue keeping races and racers together.

Trust the confidence that will unfold. That energy is guiding you to the exact path that could change your life forever.

- I am struggling with the courage to attempt new things
- I am finding it difficult to demand things such as a raise, clarification, or promotion
- I feel timid and tongue-tied
- I cannot do things alone
- I cannot stand and present in front of people
- I am not confident enough to start building another life
- I am not confident enough to reveal opinions I believe in
- I cannot refuse requests from others
- I feel I should please those around me
- **I am afraid of running the race I adore**

If that is what comes to your mind upon hearing the word "confidence," then I believe it is a must to consider this:

- Confidence is our lamplight amid turbulent times
- Confidence pulls us to engage and mingle
- Confidence pushes us to stand for our identities and truth
- Confidence helps us better cope with the current changes
- Confidence creates a different sort of worldview: a charismatic view
- Confidence is the power we run our own races with

The Potent Confidence Fuels:

#1 Fuel: Self-Thoughts: Think confidence to be confident: Ensure wiring thoughts that indicate you're good enough, adequate, and regulated. That you're doing good and can unchain all that is limiting you. That you're liberated and can stand and voice your opinions without fear.

#2 Fuel: Clear Vision: Imagine a racer riding a horse at a high speed with all senses covered and just heading somewhere unidentified. Will he be self-confident about the direction and consequences? I doubt.

The same thing goes for life and its direction. Knowing where to go in life is a confident move in itself. It gives that inner sense of reassurance and regulation.

#3 Fuel: Fearlessness: There is no room for fear with this fuel: Going where one feels afraid the most is the gateway to end all sorts of blocks. Hug your fears.

Doing it means ending it.

#4 Fuel: Faith in God: The confident racer knows that he is protected and supported wherever he goes. He knows that everything happens in a manner of sequence.

He has to do his part and leave the rest to the divine providence.

#5 Practice and Preparation: "Putting in the hour." Confidence is grown through action: Go after your dreams. If you don't go after that, your confidence will start to erode.

That can explain sometimes why the lack of doing is the problem and not the lack of knowing. There is a difference and that is what has made some people more confident than others.

When the initial stride is made, preparation comes, which protects people from pressure and fear.

Imagine stepping into an interview with zero preparation. Will the applicant go through it?

Now, imagine the opposite. Someone knowing it all before going to the meeting and prepared as if he would give the performance of his life. Won't that arm his confidence and get him through?

#6 Fuel: Bullishness: We are hard-wired to spotlight the negative and traumatic more than the positive experiences and that's ubiquitous.

One of the winning strides is when one controls his thoughts and decides to choose bullishness and thus confidence in adversities.

#7 Fuel: Potential Pleaser: Confidence gets fortified when the person shifts his focus and intention from people to place it all on his potential. Things he admires and trusts he can be brilliant at, even if they seem to be ridiculous and trivial to others.

So, the less he cares about others, the more dedicated and surer of himself he becomes.

#8 Fuel: Independence: We build self-trust when we do and navigate things ourselves: The knowledge and experiences, the feeling that no one else is around and the compulsion to manage with both possible and impossible aspects, the freedom of discovering, learning and unleashing is all an excursion toward confidence.

What self-reliance can teach us, dependence cannot.

#9 Fuel: Standing for a Different Stand: Standing for a different road means standing for the inner truth and guarding whatever is aligned with it. Choosing to march on that path less traveled even if that means standing alone is not that simple as it seems.

Expect it all from a confident person because he's certain that he can create wonders.

#10 Fuel: Knowing the Vulnerabilities: Someone knowing and accepting his vulnerabilities, can neither be conquered nor defeated. It's a fact. He won't feel unvalued because he knows what should be improved and finetuned. He believes that no one is perfect and with a bit of effort, he can climb mountains.

WOULD YOU DARE TO RUN YOUR OWN RACE?

I have immensely enjoyed talking and revealing to you the hard-learned lessons that life taught me. I've felt authentic and extremely pleased telling you about my everyday fights which are not for nothing.

I have shared a lot of what I know about how you can run your own race and firmly believe that you can become your own fearless, confident, and bold racer. I am bullish on this: You're going to start living your life abundantly and bountifully.

There is an indomitable and peerless fighter within you ready to knuckle down and go through fire and water, earth and heaven to get there. I feel it because my intuition never lies.

It doesn't matter if your race has been taken from you or doesn't seem to be as perfect as you desire it to be. It doesn't matter if you are an amateur and know nothing about running. Your destiny is malleable and you can make it work the other way.

So, don't think that you cannot do anything about it right now because you definitely can.

What matters is this: It's never too late to start over and learn and maybe relearn how to run.

I find this saying by Richard Bach to be very powerful "Don't believe what your eyes are showing you. All they show is a limitation. Look within your understanding. Find out what you already know and you will see the way to fly."

Follow your heart instead. Trust it as you always do.

Most importantly, I hope that you've come to know that your life doesn't just work like that. It's your job and accountability to have every role covered. You're the commander, the engine and fuel. You are the protagonist of your race. No one else but you.

So, keep it safe. Keep it cherished and celebrated. Keep it splendid. Keep it worthy of being remembered. Keep it elated to be lived every day. Keep it luminous. Keep it focused and unbreakable. Keep it always exciting as an adventure.

And before I leave you on the end of our journey, here's another nugget of advice:

What matters is your self-actualization and gratification which again I am not equating with having a flawless record. Trust me, I am ahead of the unhealthy perfectionism game because there are no perfect human beings. It's about finding a meaning to a life that is important to you. Running your race is a continual process of becoming rather than a seamless state one reaches of a "happily ever after." It's about eagerly attaining those peak experiences along the ride in your unique way because you're unique and so is your race.

Keep your feet straight in the stirrup, your heels down, and enjoy the ride.

Warning!

"Nawres, you should have known. You have a competitive knowledge and wisdom. You are someone who reads and is supposed to be aware. Why did you fail to change? Why did you resist the transformation you truly deserve?"

There are so many things that I read and felt like I could conquer the world and take myself very far, to wake up the next day with this: "I did it again. I am still stuck."

I carried with the spirit of change but not enough daring to function in it. I wholeheartedly wanted to create that radical transformation, but I wasn't clear or ready for the time and effort I would put in.

Who else could I point fingers at or blame? No one.

It was a dereliction from my side. I knew that I had just placed a "strikethrough" in my journal.

I knew that my old-restricted self who used to stagnate and dramatize living won then. It appeared so often because no one else but me opened the gate and allowed her to make the mess it desired.

I was operating at the surface level.

It may be surprising to say that loud and proud, but worthwhile to make you understand this:

That beast within you won't be unleashed unless you start exercising all you've covered either in my book or so many others.

The life design master classes and mentors you've placed your money on are not a magic bullet.

You've got to be the magician. Change is easy, your willingness is what should be focused on.

I don't want you to be here just to accumulate information and go write it down in your colorful notebook. Using the tools provided, I want you to take action on the change you've been seeking for long. You have already wasted enough opportunities and time, so why waste more?

So, I need you to know this: Renovation won't happen overnight because great things take time. You make small changes every day, and one day you're a changed person.

There will be those moments and challenges when you feel like nothing is working and it is taking you ages.

The trouble is that most people think that they have tried every possible way and still failed, thus poisoning their internal belief system and ending up affecting the whole process. Wrong. Wrong. Wrong.

The special sauce is this: You've got to build a muscle of consistency. For your ride to hit the mountains, you've got to be ruthlessly committed when it comes to your revision, practice, and training.

Yeah. The thought of integrating into the ride is frightening but definitely gratifying.

More About My Life-Giving Thoughts

Relationships Are like Airplane Tickets

I base this chapter on a core principle I believe in, a compromising must that goes: **Know your worth**.

Anything that doesn't have a title, clarity, or target, doesn't have worth.

I am never sure whether it's better to be alone for the rest of your life or be with someone just for the sake of being, but I am absolutely sure that it is not a great thought to be part of a relationship that doesn't have a label. That's heading nowhere.

For a start, you might think that your plan is to give yourself some assurance, balance, and a feeling of belonging, but you're not realizing how messy and unpredictable such a personal experience can be.

You're not seeing that it can drain your feelings, leaving you with nothing literally to bounce back on. You're not aware that you're giving away your human rights.

To put it differently, you're not accepting your limitations. On the contrary, you are broadening them up. You're making it more difficult for yourself to cope with serious mental and emotional torture. That means navigating a huge wave of sullen, despondent, and depressed thoughts for the rest of your life. To carry a very heavy baggage all along not knowing where to jump next.

The point I am illustrating is this: being "unlabeled" will cost you a heavy bill. And you can't and won't fake it for long because deep down, I know that your guilt will not leave you in peace.

It might seem surprising to say this, but even settling for a relationship requires good planning. You need to ask yourself questions such as:

"What can I get out of this relationship?", "Where is this relationship taking me?", "Is it aligning with the race I am running?", "Is it making me feel worthy?", "Am I being a second option?", "Am I getting by?", "What can I do about it?", "Am I truly happy?", "What do I want?"...

What's the perfect practice with clear boundaries and zero tolerance for any sort of ambiguous connections is that you have finite lines. That you know what's on you and what's for you.

No one knows your worth but yourself. Once that is done, everything else can take a hike.

For whatever relationship you take in life, take this chapter as an early warning sign. I really hope you do.

The Butterfly Mindset

[This is the chapter I would never skip].

"I want this. Oh no, I want that. I am purchasing the red shoes for sure. But I bought the green ones instead. I am resigning. I changed the plan. I am remaining for some more time."

That's often perceived as the butterfly mindset which won't keep you running for long.

It's the one mentality that keeps you looking for new things on days when you have to make something out of your current situation first. It won't allow you to increase the effort and bombproof what's presently within the reach.

What you're doing is distracting yourself by yourself. You're allowing what's superfluous to come through and have the vision that requires a peerless ability to concentrate. Yes. You can be very good at bringing new ideas and launching things, but very bad at finishing them. You get tired and move on quickly, and that's what generates passivity.

I know so many people thinking up new ideas, always excited and prepared for new experiences, but following up on what's happening is a no-way task for them.

The best advice I can give you is to stick with one single idea and give it your all. Step by step, day by day.

The more focused you are, the easier it becomes for you to get the right answers and make the correct decisions.

As you become more in control of your thoughts, it will transform how you interact and run your race.

Don't Let the Label Label You

People have found themselves married to unwanted partners because saying "no" to their families is a disgrace.

People have found themselves being pitched to run studies and occupations because an unnegotiable decision has already been made for them.

People have found themselves giving up on awe-incredible ideas because the mob said possibilities and large goals are just for those with gifted intellect and allure.

People have found themselves seeing life from the perspective of age just because "it's too late" is all that is heard.

People have found themselves unable to see life further than the front door, being told that stepping out of the safe harbor is uncomfortable and unpleasant.

People have found themselves losing that burst of passion because of being told that "what-if challenges and change are impossible."

Those are the same people who have grown sluggish, searching for themselves.

Those are the same people who have lost their true talents and identities.

Those are the same people who wished on their deathbeds that they had run their races.

Are you most people?

With that in mind, don't let the label label you.

Know When the Dog Is Dead

This brief and deep chapter pays to think now:

Some relationships aren't going to last. Some occupations aren't going to be yours. Some projects aren't going to work and succeed. Some doors aren't going to open for you. Some dreams aren't going to be fulfilled. Some stories aren't going to end happily and some hopes are going to fade away for no reason.

What's special is a good racer who knows when he has to stride back and just stop draining his time and power. He knows when he has to stop trying and move. He **knows when the dog is dead.**

Here's your shield: detachment. You've got to pull the "detach handle" and be ruthless in letting go.

I know that I am streamlining this while moving on from that toxic relationship that broke my heart and those many doors being shut in front of my face. It wasn't as simple as it sounds to walk away from that feeling of being fooled around or played up. It was so hard not to think that I was a failure or pathetic. It really took the wind out of my sails. Yet, trust me: sometimes, you've got to learn how to shrug and just go without even saying that you're going. You don't have to leave a further notice or blame. You've got to save your energy because your race needs you the most. It needs you before anybody else. And as they say: "You've got to put your oxygen mask first before assisting others."

It takes so long to move on mentally and emotionally. Leave it there and get going on your next big exciting step and distant horizons. Proceed to what's thrilling, bearing in mind that there has to be some good hard inner work.

Sitting there on the fence drained to make a move won't heal you. It won't make you a startlingly sublime and brave racer. But I am positive that you're a mover, high-flyer, and go-getter. I am buoyant that you're unstoppable.

Take That Business Card

Strangers are not as bad as our parents taught us.

Here's why: That person you're avoiding looking straight in the eye and saying "Hello, I would love to introduce myself" might be the one turning your career into a mind-boggling one.

That person you're running from thinking that he wants to bother or kidnap you in the worst-case scenarios might be the one believing in your projects and introducing you to the world.

And that business card you're hesitating to take might be the way out to that step you're dying to take.

So often, incredible success comes from unexpected people and scopes. It comes from random encounters.

We all do it. We all think that they don't fit and nothing is important there. We all think that they are a waste of time.

We get so worked up over our one big plan that we lose sight of the fact that we can do better and bring what wasn't brought to the table before.

We were all once and maybe still too single-minded and caught up in what we think is the most important thing.

This chapter is not a contradiction to the previous ones where I am encouraging you to be intentional and head straight.

Yet, here's the thing: Randomness is not about going aimlessly without any focus.

You can still be committed to your highest standards and at the same time think differently and look at success in the most diverse ways.

What I have come to understand is that real success is not normal. It is not about logic and practicality.

So, you need to avoid the straitjacket thinking. You need to lift your head and take randomness into account. You need to look out of your circle and cast a wider one.

You've got to put that book or phone down and talk to the person sitting next to you in a coffee shop or on an airplane.

And what are you going to say to them? That's easy.

Anything that might help you become and do better.

The more you talk, the more credit you'll get back. The more ideas, suggestions, concepts, and directions you'll gain.

To fathom and implement such an approach is to become a cutting-edge sort of racer.

Still thinking? I beg you not. Go take that business card.

The Rollercoaster

[Being more transparent in this chapter.]

Things don't seem to go simple and straight sometimes: turning me here and there, left and right, leaving me in the middle of the trip, lost.

I am meant for rollercoaster rides. I think!
I couldn't find a better example than this to relate. Honest. That's riding. It has to be uncomfortable, tiring, frightening, sensational, and delightful. It has to hold the feet up. I forgot that the undesirable rides are blessings sometimes that perhaps just need to be raised and then polished.

The bottomless and ultimate encouragement is that triumph is a feeling, not a title. To reach or not. To be appreciated or not. You're a good racer. You need to bear that the tiniest achievements matter a lot because a true and passionate effort deceives none. Trust that.

You don't have to question the faith, but the conclusion. You need not judge or pressure yourself but understand and outline the conditions.

Life is a rollercoaster, dear racers. Just ride it. And if the feet are on the ground, then you're not riding.

Thoughts From Maldives

[This chapter did speak to my soul. I hope it speaks to your soul too.]

Here I am in the tropical nirvana of Maldives, reveling up and getting my heart racing and jumping in excitement. I can feel powerful magic on hearing the peaceful rustling sea waves, seeing the seagulls soaring above, and sensing the hotness of sand with the roughness of its little living things.

Obviously, I'm happier with nature. Adventure seems to be everywhere.

And the aroma of this place. Oh, it is the aroma of freedom and euphoria.

...So much positive and epic change. I deem!

This astonishing island managed to move me in a manner that I had never felt before. That's no lie. And it made me write:

Humbleness Is Free:
The air smells authentic and unpretentious over here. Brilliant smiles are all I can see everywhere: Staff from the resort to the tourists, everyone is greeting and helping each other from the heart: caring less about being different and more about showing some respect and care.

And so, humbleness is simple and small, but it passes. It's effective. It's free.

Solitude Is a Solace:
Entering into a mood of closeness and engagement with the self solves strife, and declutters our thoughts. It dispels an endless

reserve of optimism, hope, and jubilation, that other tools may be unable to do.

Fasting From the Hectic Life Is Important:
Being stress-free is the adopted slogan here: I can see people reading and nurturing their brains whilst being careless about media and digital gadgets.

Some are diving into the clear sea, and others are having fun with frisbees in the sea sports area.

Others are just sunbathing and getting a red-bronze golden tone.

We are all here to escape from our stressful lives and get refueled, recovered, and revived.

Breathing Into Nature Is Reviving:
The Lord is splendid and nature is stupendous.

Nature is so different here: the beach is pristine, the air is clean, and greenery is all around with fragrant plants and leaf-tailed chameleons.

The natural aura is so light that we can't but heal, and feel happier and healthier as we breathe into it.

What Can Be Double-Edged

"Don't rush. You're only twenty-three. You're still young and have a whole wide future ahead of you." An advice that I often receive as I reveal the passion I have and sound like an "idealistic dreamer."

Whenever I go revaluating it: I wonder, is it a guidance that one can find room for or just turn plugging his ears shut to?

I get their meaning: Don't miss out on the present fantastic moments for probing the future. And don't hasten things to happen earlier. There is a right time for everything. Enjoy your living instead.

I agree. Life should be balanced and relished. Definitely, not strict.

After careful consideration, I found the guidance double-edged and holding a delicate line that could serve or ruin me.

Here I explain: If you remain postponing palpable potentials, truthful relationships, and intriguing scopes, assuming there is adequate time and a particular age to be, then let the nagging guilt be your lifetime partner.

The bottom line is this: Putting in the hour and doing the absolute best is not going to hamper your youth [if they see it as a matter of age because I don't], but instead set it on a thrilling gratification.

I hope you get the point.

What Life Taught Me and Schools Didn't

I must have told you somewhere in my books that I didn't finish my education. That I have never believed in certificates.

Coming from a family that worships education, the decision was hard. Though I vividly remember that I had been one of the best pupils throughout those years. Being there before anybody else, taking the first row, and being ready to ask questions. I was always keen to be the best in my class, to be the good and well-prepared girl, and to show to my instructors that I loved competing with my classmates.

The intriguing thing is that those traits have remained in me and with them I have been navigating my journey as a self-taught person.

I trusted life to be my school and best teacher. And I am elated to do so. I was positive then and still am. And this positivity can make me better, more rounded, and more knowledgeable.

I know this chapter is pretty shocking and kindly don't get me wrong here. I don't think that you need to leave your studies. What I am saying here is that if you have a deep desire to own your race, you've got to realize that running is more about real-life skills and less about those bunch of certificates you're hanging on the wall.

Wondering what life taught me and schools didn't. Here I go:

1. Working bloody hard on my potential as I do for my

homework and tests
   2. Following my intuition more often
   3. Shining lights on my talents and gifts and staying in the process of making them real
   4. Considering hobbies as a good long-term career
   5. The science of willpower
   6. Thinking independently
   7. Conducting a self-positive talk daily
   8. Being my everyday hero
   9. Controlling my thoughts and defeating doubts
   10. Asking "What happened to me" instead of "What's wrong with me"
   11. The importance of working for myself and being an entrepreneur
   12. Never saying yes to everything
   13. Sticking by my small dreams and growing them over time
   14. Setting up a strong culture
   15. Having a mission in life to wake up for
   16. Being original and standing firmly for my mysterious marking
   17. Seeing failure as a win
   18. Being prepared for pleasure and pain
   19. To focus on the excursion but not the results

It's my true belief that if you step just one step, one step only outside of what they have taught us, you'll recognize that there is another completely different world that we still know less than nothing about.

Grabbing Chances

To step the step, you've got to grab the chance first. Isn't it? "Have you ever wondered how small the chances were that you would be born? If just one thing in history had changed, just one of your millions of ancestors had not crossed paths the exact way they did, then you would not exist. You would never have to live a single day."

Such a deep and great thought has grabbed my attention from the movie Love Wedding Repeat.

It has made me contemplate those chances that appear in our lives all the time. Chances that sometimes get neglected and rejected out of disqualification, fear, and unawareness.

Let me give the example of getting the scope of exercising in a different fitness center so you learn better from stronger coaches and athletes.

…The choice of shifting to another urban area, getting into a different business, and then bringing your career to a higher level.

Or the prospect of saluting a stranger on an elevator and ending up with him becoming your dearest and most inspiring friend.

See… those are the same chances that can get your glorious unseen talents revealed and perceived. The same chances that can get you pushed into gear and step out in the world as a luminous and shimmering individual. Chances that can make you peerless and of incremental growth and immense strength.

Let us be candid and confess that a meaningful life is about grabbing and embracing those small opportunities.

Hold then upon the chance of appreciating, supporting, expanding, attracting, shining, rivaling, learning, and gaining expertise. The chance of soaring greater and becoming better and nobler.

And so, refuse to stand still and grab each chance that can help you run your race.

Dive Into a Real Story

Being a dreamer, possessing an unsurpassed dedication and holding the most daring hopes.

His deepest belongings and thoughts are so true for him because real momentums and brains cannot be pretended.

Sure, he has luminous talents and a rousing potential to unleash them. He believes in the inner gratification and richness that lasts. That true significance of being.

"I can," is the one thing he has been telling himself.

"You've dropped it, I imagine. Your mind... You said then becoming an author and motivating the public."

"You mean selling delusions to people and robbing them of their time and hope? Please be real! You cannot build such a career and secure an income. Scripting itself is pure rubbish and disappointment is ahead," admitted the scoffer in a sardonic and teasing tone.

Though the dreamer felt the need to respond, nothing came out. His rational mind needed to trust that, but his heart and potent instinct could not.

The ridicule made his chest feel hotter. "Fit in... Fit in..." continued the scoffer.

Dampening the atmosphere and attempting to get him dragged to the trades of impossibilities, did not impact the dreamer. The ideals too did not become less important.

The opposite happened instead. His smile radiated more, and a tinge of sharper confidence appeared.

Lifting his head, he said, "I can" and left.

He is not the sort of person who stops because of a scoffer. He is not the sort of person to shatter a promise. He is a one-jump ahead of the game. In that case, his dream has meaning.

I am illustrating a point here: Daring dreamers too pass through difficult ridiculers and festering thoughts. But the boldest don't stop.

Rich in Time

There are too many horror stories of people giving away their lifetimes for excuses, loitering, and indolence.

They go unzipping themselves in this false belief: "I can do it tomorrow." Later to mask any grief they might have felt with buying trivialities. Ones that do not touch the soul, for they are external and apish.

And eventually to be on their deathbeds confessing: "I was once a fortunate man, but I lost it."

Time is a heaped-up treasure. And he who shuts his eyes of such blessing is poor.

In this what is the difference between him who lives three days and him who lives three generations? It's a time investment.

Take my words please: No longer let this be a slave, no longer be pulled by the strings like a marionette to how the majority is mistreating such gems. Still remember that no man loses any other life than this which he lives now, for nothing can compensate for it.

With every second wasted, the chance of running your race shrinks, and that's when the world can work against you.

A great racer is one who never fritters away time on anything that doesn't move him forward, who believes in living in the best way, and pursuing a necessary pursuit of efficiency.

So, do you have time? Yes, you do. Why then don't you use it? For if time is money, what other wealth could you wish for?

Time Is Time, Every Time

I am not a poet, but my heart is lifting at these simple thoughts to be jotted.

> Time isn't there in the past
> or in the future.
> Time is right around.
> It's here within the reach.
> Squandering it is unease,
> and non-earning it is hard to believe.
> The slaughtering chair of guilt is a deem
> for which I put on the most confident voice,
> and write procrastination is a thief.
> Time is a blessing.
> Time is a pressing.
> Time is time, every time.

Because I Am Very Human. I Confess

[A really raw chapter]

As I write this small piece for you, I am reflecting on a glorious quietude, savoring a cup of intense coffee, and connecting with the human residing in me... The authentic being that has it all.

I commit minor if not tremendous errors.

I find the thunderous times to be rough and tough to cope with, and thus get messed up and lost.

I fathom fate being unfaithful sometimes.

I feel irritable and void for not attaining all I yearn for.

I imagine dreadful scenarios and develop frights.

I go double-minded and lose my devoted faith.

I reflect much and forget to relish the glorious present.

I condemn the self for resting and not being fruitful.

I get uncomfortable and insecure about initiating a fresh start.

I crave atonement, praise, and appreciation.

I conceal scars and wounds behind a thrilling charisma.

I tend to be demotivated by rejections, failures, and tons of tries.

I overdo and push things to end up overburdened. I lose track and feel like doing nothing sometimes.

...I have all of this inside me because I am very human. I confess...

As a confession, I have been finding power in congruency and authenticity.

In a world that has morphed accepting the real self [regarding its mess] into shame and powerlessness, and focused on the outward instead of inward stamina, I call you to reconnect and salute the incredible being within you... accept, filter, and re-engineer it, and then go out into the world to run your own race.

Smashing the Safe Harbor

In a cut-throat culture that suggests common sense and safe games, it costs nothing to remain the same and chill on the sofa. It's simple and super easy to sit in a pit of misery, averageness, passivity, mediocrity, and stagnation. Isn't it?

The buffer or safe harbor I am planning in this chapter can be seen through getting that salary or allow me to say "drug" they give you to forget about your dreams. It can be seen through having the same breakfast, adopting the same typical way of thinking, running the same position, believing in, and confronting the same habits for decades. The time says it all. And I can relate.

"SAME"! The term itself is so comfortable. So peaceful. So common. So quiet. It sounds like a nirvana indeed: so perfect and happy but feels closely massacring.

To be blunt: the grounded life is good. I guess we all desire to have a stable and organized life. We all want to feel secure (as per Abraham Maslow and his hierarchy of needs) I am not encouraging you to throw yourselves in danger and give up on your current securities or even pushing you to compare yourselves with others. We're not competing here, so let's not blend things.

The message I am trying to offer you is that your or my comfort zones won't fuel our rise and transform our game. It will keep us paralyzed to change. Even when the signs indicate that it's time to take a different path, your cozy version will concede and reject that. It will do the absolute possible to always push away what is best for you and to keep what's good because it has its own true and false set of opinions. It has its own rules, terminology, inconvertible stories, and allies.

It's a whole complete gate of repetition and perfunctory behavior. Once entered, the man becomes belligerent and hostile in front of the smallest challenges. He becomes enfeebled and so leveraged. He ends up forgetting about his special life and starts living fully in society, so he follows the usual trail. The dormant one.

The raw truth is this:

You don't have to waste twenty years of your life thinking that it's all about comfort. You don't have to feel regret and mental torture to understand that.

And so, I pray you believe in this: if it's not challenging, it's not changing.

Leaving you on this note:

Your safe harbor won't get you the character of a racer. Act the part. Do the part and cut it out.

To the Mental Escapes, I Am Indebted

I just needed to take some time off. I am going for it now.

I must share: Life is hectic again and that is a red alert not to be ignored and thus grabbing the chance to be in Tanzania feels far more fulfilling. I know the trip would change me a bit. I feel it is a door-kicking opportunity to relax mentally.

Being in the arms of Zanzibar, sleeping on Nungwi beach, reading "When You Get the Change" by Emma Lord, listening to afro music, staring out at the handmade sea boats, and sunbathing.

Art, peace, and simplicity. It's the "Hakuna Matata" life. And because each mental escape can bring a bunch of gains,

I am indebted for:

- Scaling the inner influence and heightening its impact
- Bringing quietude
- Unleashing greater ideas
- Fireproofing the momentum
- Envisioning the template
- Remaining adaptable in the moment of assortment
- The closure and absolute muse
- Healing a strife
- Remaining focused and sharpened
- Cleaning the mental debris
- Generating insights and detecting opportunities

- Understanding and finding a contentment that lasts

Oh, Zanzi Zanzi, you've had my heart.

Don't You Worry? I Am Beyond Possible

Don't be bothered about me. I am stupendous.
I am all enlivened, and so that life is brighter here.
For the diligent and believer, I am devoted and promising.
For the resolute, I am honest and determined.
To come and reach me, the universe has the right timing.
Things happen in a manner of sequence, so let there be freedom from uncertainties.
You've been striving and doing the best for me.
Your sincere desire and devotion are all I breathe through and consider the most.
I can see that no fact is unimportant to me. I feel the groove inside.
For that, I am not far.
I am here, waiting.
I am close and approachable,
I am beyond possible.

    Yours,
    The Future

Rejected but Never Squashed Up

"Rejection." I believe we all have experienced it over those rising pursuits we have promised ourselves we would do.

It is that disappointment that irritates, infuriates, and triggers even more self-doubts… leading to the bravado to fade away and the white flag to be waved at times.

But then, hold on!

If we examine the life of every fantastic winning racer on this planet, we'll find refusal being a part of his or her excursion.

Enrico Caruso had become the greatest opera singer of his age at a time when his teacher denied it and left him distraught with "You can't sing."

Arthur Ashe, the first African American to gain induction into the Tennis Hall of Fame, couldn't go to the training institute due to racism.

Oprah Winfrey, the most inspiring TV host, and producer, was rejected because people saw in her no potential, but her gender and color.

J. K. Rowling, the writer of the life-treasured Harry Potter novel, turned down multiple publishers for years, fighting for her ideas.

Charles Dickens, the thrilling English novelist, and legend of the Victorian Era, before receiving his initial publication approval had his stories rebuffed one after the other.

Robin Sharma, the top author, and leadership expert in the world received a rejection letter on his first read ever *The Monk Who Sold His Ferrari* from the publisher labeling it "pure garbage." The titan didn't give up and the same masterpiece ended up being the first best seller to change the lives of millions.

And the list goes on...

Some days you will feel like a sad karaoke song, looking at your most audacious dreams getting shattered and squashed up to begin losing the zest of dreaming big. Yeah, we may have lost a lot and thought foolishly that it was over. But hell no, we're just getting started. And so just because you get rejected doesn't mean you should not remain a delightful dreamer, a beam of light.

The game can still be changed. I think you'll value the fact that disappointment, torment, and restfulness must not step in your way and so we must forget about the disheartening side to begin seeing what's uplifting.

Don't know how? Here's a defensive mechanism:

Accept the Rejection:

It is arduous to accept and not feel a thing. I have been through that stage too. Yet, here is the thing to be appreciated: rejection switches off your engine of optimism, and shuts your eyes to see the equivalent profits. You need to assume it is a gain and not a failure or you'll remain where you are for decades, languishing.

Shouldn't then we be understanding and tolerant?

Applaud Yourself:

The world is filled with people who do less and talk much, and because you are unlike them and have the take-action mindset that doesn't believe either in magic or fortune, applaud yourself for starting and trying. Now and ever...

Trust this: It takes uncommon and substantial courage to take one single step to run the race. And you get that.

See the Upside of Your Downside:
Everything happens for a reason and is malleable. I am a firm believer in that.

If it is the case of working a bit harder, then see it as a chance to increment your current aptitudes and release the untapped ones.

If you have done your best and gone through earth and heaven, wait as the universe is arranging something greater for you.

If another trail has to be traversed, approach it with this great observation "Sometimes rejection in life is redirection."

Trust the Providence:
Remain a deep believer and be free from uncertainties. Everything running in your life is controlled and monitored. God is there for us, seeing scenarios we cannot see and hearing conversations we cannot hear. He has the wisest control to do things. Why then are you so vexed?

One more point to say straight out: as long as you are diligent, benevolent, candid, and passionate, blessings and attainments are forever in your favor.

I am very positive that regardless of the denial you are facing, you still have the agency to promote and voice your most decisive and resolute dreams.

Reckless Enough to Say No

Reckless enough to say no to:

- negativity and poisonous mediocrity
- gossipy conversations
- mistreatment and disrespect
- a ten-second reel of people dancing
- distractions and interruptions
- any reappearance of past experiences or rapports
- the old and distrustful habits
- the fear and self-uncertainties
- sluggishness and anti-peaceful environments
- the ritual of collecting more and being less
- whatever is unwanted and untruthful to the core values

Because within each "no" resides a gain of well-being…

The Cheerful Child

The thirst for artful places is deep and enduring for me. I find museums to be impressive and inspirational at best. I see that we can invigorate and set our aura on fire with enthusiasm.

At the Louvre AUH, I found a French handcrafted sculpture named "The Cheerful Child" by Claude Francois Attiret that got me beguiled and enthralled. It is simple, and potent, can get us connected to the 18th luminous epoch, and reengage with the cheerful child residing within us.

The cheerful child that loves venturing out, and can cross paths, unafraid of falling and lapses.

Having a giant unstoppable momentum to snatch opportunities.

Befriending life and savoring each moment; unstressed about the future.

Expressing immense gratitude and planting ecstasy everywhere.

Being pure-hearted and lending a helping hand to whoever is in need.

Believing in magic, trusting, and creating it.

Listening to the instinct and bringing rise to discoveries.

Deeming the truth and releasing feelings without fear.

Being curious and determined to inquire and learn.

Finding bliss within a simple living and small offerings.

Voicing that grand feeling of being whatever we want to be with boldness.

For that cheerful child inside us, let's forever be it. Let's forever protect it.

Are You Feeling Lost?

For that clumsy and uncomfortable feeling that hits us at times.
    Do you have the financial freedom, resources, dream occupation, and car?
    Are you passionate about life?
    Do you have an audacious vision?
    Have you completed your vision board filled with goals?
    Did you succeed in business?
    Do you have an incredible partner?
    Is your psychological immune system solid?
    Do you have a supportive community?
    Do you have a family that always wraps you with unconditional love and care?
    Do you mark all those questions with "yes" and still feel lost? Do you have it all but can't point your finger to what's missing knowing that something is bothering you; you sense it in the core of your being. Do you cry more than you laugh and do not understand who you truly are?
    Training my whole life for this: No human being on this earth has figured it all out. Nobody's ride is impeccable because we're very human.
    One thing I know: the race has to continue.

The Lifetime Lessons My First Book Taught Me

1. Sincere effort deceives none.
2. Great things require time. Lots of time.
3. Patience is a blessing.
4. There is a price tag for accomplishments and that's certain.
5. Time and not resources matters the most.
6. The harder it gets, the stronger the dedication becomes.
7. The higher the dream, the more difficult rituals you need.
8. Sometimes trauma isn't the end. It's the beginning to soar.
9. Procrastination is the scariest robber. Smash it.
10. You don't need to see the result. Start instead.
11. Creation comes from a deep isolation.
12. You need to do what most people are unwilling to do: push the envelope.
13. Mastery is all about deliberate practice.
14. Doing our best is not sometimes the best. Hard work is a journey in itself.
15. Deciding to do the difficult things is a giant conquest.
16. Practice, self-trust, and momentum management are the fuels.
17. Genius is not gifted. Genius is gained.
18. Impossible itself says "I'm possible."
19. The true dream presupposes a change of mind, a change of performance.
20. God shows you the dream but never the plan.
21. Small practices lead to terrific results.
22. The restrained capacities become the repressed emotional

hurdles.

23. Don't be median. Be distinguished and bring in the special touch.

24. Art is scary, yet gratifying.

25. If we couldn't do it yesterday, it doesn't mean we can't do it today.

Find more about RUN IT and our programs which I base on my RCUP philosophy at: run-it.ae

Together, Let's Run It!